A Sports Odyssey

In the series *Sporting*, edited by Amy Bass

ALSO IN THIS SERIES:

Kaitlin Pericak, *Body Factory: Exploiting University Athletes' Healthcare for Profit in the Training Room*

Samir Chopra, *The Evolution of a Cricket Fan: My Shapeshifting Journey*

Rebecca Joyce Kissane and Sarah Winslow, *Whose Game? Gender and Power in Fantasy Sports*

Charles K. Ross, *Mavericks, Money, and Men: The AFL, Black Players, and the Evolution of Modern Football*

Yago Colás, *Ball Don't Lie! Myth, Genealogy, and Invention in the Cultures of Basketball*

Thomas P. Oates and Zack Furness, eds., *The NFL: Critical and Cultural Perspectives*

David L. Andrews and Michael L. Silk, eds., *Sporting and Neoliberalism: Politics, Consumption, and Culture*

David Wangerin, *Distant Corners: American Soccer's History of Missed Opportunities and Lost Causes*

Zack Furness, *One Less Car: Bicycling and the Politics of Automobility*

Michael Ezra, *Muhammad Ali: The Making of an Icon*

Thomas Hauser, *The Boxing Scene*

David Wangerin, *Soccer in a Football World: The Story of America's Forgotten Game*

Grant Farred, *Long Distance Love: A Passion for Football*

Tommie Smith, *Silent Gesture: The Autobiography of Tommie Smith*

Grant Farred

A Sports Odyssey

My Ithaca Journal

TEMPLE UNIVERSITY PRESS
Philadelphia • *Rome* • *Tokyo*

TEMPLE UNIVERSITY PRESS
Philadelphia, Pennsylvania 19122
tupress.temple.edu

Copyright © 2025 by Temple University—Of The Commonwealth System
 of Higher Education
All rights reserved
Published 2025

Library of Congress Cataloging-in-Publication Data

Names: Farred, Grant author
Title: A sports odyssey : my Ithaca journal / Grant Farred.
Description: Philadelphia : Temple University Press, 2025. | Series:
 Sporting | Includes bibliographical references and index. | Summary:
 "This book reflects on the local, temporal, and arbitrary nature of
 commitment, affiliation, and fandom. The author diarizes a period in the
 spring of 2024 in which sports mediate his ties to his family, his
 occupational institution, and his global identity"—
 Provided by publisher.
Identifiers: LCCN 2025003095 (print) | LCCN 2025003096 (ebook) | ISBN
 9781439926949 cloth | ISBN 9781439926956 paperback | ISBN 9781439926963 pdf
Subjects: LCSH: Farred, Grant—Diaries | Sports—Psychological aspects
 | Liverpool Football Club | Cornell Big Red (Basketball team) | Sports
 spectators—New York (State)—Ithaca—Biography | Ithaca
 (N.Y.)—Biography
Classification: LCC GV706.4 .F278 2025 (print) | LCC GV706.4 (ebook) | DDC
 796.092 [B]—dc23/eng/20250417
LC record available at https://lccn.loc.gov/2025003095
LC ebook record available at https://lccn.loc.gov/2025003096

The manufacturer's authorized representative in the EU for product safety is
Temple University Rome, Via di San Sebastianello, 16, 00187 Rome RM, Italy
(https://rome.temple.edu/).
tempress@temple.edu

9 8 7 6 5 4 3 2 1

This book is dedicated to:
Brian Earl: basketball coach responsive to the world,
generous human being, and, importantly, a man possessed,
mercifully, of just the right amount of sardonic edge;
Zeke: a tough, combative competitor, the ultimate team player,
and, much as he will demur, a basketball player destined to be a coach;
And, finally, to
Jürgen Norbert Klopp: a man of the Scouser people,
a man true to the spirit of Liverpool Football
Club. Aufwiedersehn. Danke, for Trent above all else.
For Trent Alexander-Arnold, Jürgen.

The best lack all conviction, while the worst
Are full of passionate intensity.
> W. B. Yeats, "The Second Coming."[1]

CONTENTS.

Acknowledgments. xiii

Introduction: My Ithaca Journal. 1
The Decision, One That Lacks a Clear Explanation. 11
Nature Abhors a Vacuum. 18
The Ivies: Three Tours of Duty. 25
January 26, 2024: A Day to Remember. 29
7:30 P.M., January 26, 2024: Ezra's Starting. 35
January 27, 2024: Charles Oakley. 36
Intra-Ivy Envy. Or, Which of These Five Schools Is More Insecure about Its Ivy Status than Its Peers? Or, Only in America. 38
Class Warfare in the "Little Ivies." 41
Dartmouth, Again, Briefly. But Not for the Last Time. 43
Intra-Ivy Fraternal Tensions, Continued. 45
February 2, 2024. 47
January 27, 2024. 49
A Colored Ivy. Penn, Again. 50
January 27, 2024: Beating Princeton. 53
January 31, 2024. 54
January 27, 2024. 56

"Over-Rated."	58
11:25 A.M., January 30, 2024.	60
January 27, 2024.	61
4:45 P.M., January 27, 2024.	63
A Saturday in September 1990.	64
Brian Earl Is a Princeton Man. I Am Not a Princeton Man. Maybe Brian Earl Is Not a Princeton Man.	67
4:45 P.M., January 27, 2024.	72
1:36 P.M., January 26, 2024.	73
Lead Story on the Six O'clock News in England: January 26, 2024.	74
#20s.	75
January 27, 2024.	77
The Game after *The* Announcement.	79
January 28, 2024.	81
January 30, 2024.	82
Pep Guardiola on Sleeping Easy.	83
Pep Knows.	85
Jürgen Klopp Knows What Pep Knows. Twice Over.	88
January 31, 2024.	92
February 1, 2024.	94
1:10 P.M., February 6, 2024.	95
January 31, 2024.	97
Jürgen Klopp's Birthday.	98
1:00 P.M., February 8, 2024.	99
Ulla Sandrock.	101
February 9, 2024.	102
February 10, 2024.	104
February 11, 2024.	106
Why the Niners Made It Difficult to Root for Them.	108
Taylor Swift Puts the Fear of Electoral Defeat into MAGA.	113
The Morning After the Morning After the Morning After, the Niners Make You Happy They Lost.	116
CK, KC: As a Curse.	121
February 16, 2024.	122

"Ferret."	124
February 17, 2024.	130
8:00 P.M., February 17, 2024.	132
5:34 P.M., February 18, 2024.	134
Phil Collins.	135
8:17 P.M., February 19, 2024.	138
1:02 P.M., February 20, 2024.	139
9:15 A.M., February 27, 2024.	141
Brian Earl: Princetonian Gone Rogue?	143
7:23 P.M., February 21, 2024.	146
Winning the Ivies.	148
February 20, 2024.	150
Chris Manon.	151
Wistfulness, Regret.	153
12:45 P.M., June 1, 2019: Madrid, Spain.	155
TAA.	158
February 23, 2024.	160
10:28 A.M., February 23, 2024.	162
7:05 P.M., February 23, 2024.	163
National Anthem.	164
7:15 P.M., February 23, 2024.	166
February 25, 2024.	169
11:27 A.M., February 26, 2024.	171
1:40 P.M., March 16, 2024.	176
2:00 P.M., March 16, 2024.	177
It's Elton John Time.	178
Brian Earl's Face.	182
8:16 P.M., March 16, 2024.	184
10:56 A.M., St. Patrick's Day.	185
March 18, 2024.	186
Ivy Title Game.	188
March 20, 2024.	190
March 19, 2024.	192
You Lose Something When They're Gone.	194

The New York Knicks.	196
Bob Dylan.	198
Postscript: 9:37 A.M., March 24, 2024.	201
The Postscript's Postscript: Subtext.	202
Notes.	207
Index.	215

Acknowledgments.

Ryan Mulligan. Amy Bass.

Without these editors, this project would never have seen the light of day. Amy pointed me in the direction I needed to go from the first moment I mooted the idea of *A Sports Odyssey: My Ithaca Journal*. Ryan patiently walked me through first the bureaucratic process and then he nudged me, as he always does, into doing what was necessary.

My thanks, offered here to Amy and Ryan, are constitutively insufficient but entirely sincere. My debt to them grows.

I owe Brian Earl a singular thanks. It is he who inspired this book. He provided the spur that got me writing, but that isn't the half of it. He drew me into the orbit of the Cornell University men's basketball team. He is generous to a fault, especially in relation to Ezra, my son. He is possessed of an innovative basketball mind. He faces the moments of difficulty with poise and conviction. His sons, Dylan, Owen, and Cooper, are a delight, a relentless whirl of energy. And his wife, Jen, is as tough as they come.

I cannot tell him how much I regret his departure from Ithaca.

I am the poorer for his leaving.

Mr. Jaques, former model Cornell student, current Cornell men's head coach. You're the kind of person who makes everyone want to root for you, Mr. Jaques, me not least among them.

This is a mark of your fundamental decency.

The 2023–24 edition of the Cornell men's basketball team made of me an institutional creature, as long as it was this team that constituted the institution. To AK, Adam, Beccles, Jake, Cooper, Josh: the highlight of my day was often either watching you practice or talking with you after practice.

Guy Ragland: a man of depth, thoughtfulness (to wit: Father's Day 2024) and modesty.

Nas: Ezra wants to emulate you. I can't decide whether that's a good or bad thing. I know which way I'm inclining, but your *joie de vivre* is a marvel to behold.

Sean Hansen, the Bricklayer: the consummate team player, a man who carries his intelligence with ease.

Keller Boothby, Smooth Operator: possessed of a strong sense of self, not thrown off course by this development or that, a man who will always find the way to where it is he wants to go.

Chris Manon: a man who faces the difficulties life throws up, takes its pulse, and responds, not always in ways that appear the wisest course of action but always with a smile and a spirit that seems indomitable, regardless of the obstacles that lie ahead—or behind, for that matter.

Zeke: coach-in-training. No, born to play the game, overcome the challenges, born to be a coach, already a coach. Zeke, who took Ezra under his wing and gave him the best of Zeke. In a word, *Focus*. Zeke, who is casual about some things and deeply dedicated to what matters to him. You'll be a college coach yet, Zeke, despite your justifiable reservations. And you'll be a very good one.

Thanks to Jeremy Hartigan of Cornell University for how easy you made it to secure the images. Appreciated.

And now, the declarative moment—that moment I take issue with all those family members and friends who did not believe me when I told them that I had given up my beloved Liverpool Football Club. None of my friends believed me. So, I hope that writing *An Ithaca Sports Journal* is proof enough. It's a public statement, after all. In rough alphabetical order: Andrew, yes, it is true; B., when I call you and you tell me that you're watching the World Cup final, that's all I got; David A., I suspect that you expect that one day, soon, I'll come to my senses; David F., I find your silence around this matter slightly unnerving; Peter G., you shake your head ruefully and wonder with your trademark laugh; Jernej, your voice betrays a doubtful comprehension; Orin, I can hear the chuckle of disbelief every time we talk—like David A., you think I'm just taking a sabbatical; Danes, you feed me bits of F1 info, sure that I've never really stopped tracking Sir Lewis's fortunes.

The moment of unmasking: Ross D., Patrick G., and Wander dH., apologies, I can dissemble no more.

No one in my family really believes that this has happened. No, Juanita, I am not in the basement quietly watching. When I watched Liverpool, you knew by the sound of my voice and the often-inexcusable language that issued forth from me what I was doing.

Bug: I might yet ask for a Liverpool jersey, but it will be a throwback one. Alex: yes, I've actually done it.

Nip: I am sorry to disappoint you. But now there's more time for analyzing our New York Knicks. Be Josh Hart with a side dish of Dennis Rodman. Study history. Let's go to Japan. With Bug.

To Jürgen Klopp: for not only what you gave Liverpool Football Club, but, most importantly, how you gave yourself to us. *Vielen dank.*

And, finally, to Trent Alexander-Arnold. Thanks for that moment at the Wanda Metropolitano, June 2, 2019. You are a footballer. The sumptuousness of your passes, the likes of which I have not seen before, will remain with me always. How you pass, TAA. How you see what might be long before everyone else, on and off the pitch. I regret that I will not see you in your pomp—your later pomp, #66.

A Sports Odyssey

Introduction: My Ithaca Journal.

I'm no Greg Heffley, but, then again, who is? My son Ezra and I are both huge fans of Jeff Kinney's *Diary of a Wimpy Kid*. If you are not familiar with the diary of Wimpy Kid Extraordinaire, Greg Heffley, consider that a major gap in your cultural education. My debt to the Wimpy Kid is of such a magnitude that following the dictates of a diary, Greg Heffley style, seemed to me, on January 26, 2024, the only way to write *My Ithaca Journal*.

A Sports Odyssey: My Ithaca Journal is, then, ironically, (more) true to the journal as a literary form than Greg ever is. He opens his *Diary* with a correction: "First of all, let me get something straight: This is a JOURNAL, not a diary. I know what it says on the cover, but when Mom went out to buy this thing, I SPECIFICALLY told her to get one that didn't say 'diary' on it."[2] Despite his protestations, Greg shows himself—no matter his capitalization of the word, Dear Reader—to be only a diarist. Though I admit he is a winning and thoroughly engaging one, he's no "journalist," our Greg Heffley, certainly not in the sense that *My Ithaca Journal* is a journal. He keeps things on a day-to-day basis, recording nothing of importance; in short, he does Greg.

But the spirit of Greg is not so easily denied, as *My Ithaca Journal* is also subject to the whimsy of the day-to-day. The difference between the two journals, however, is not insignificant. In between *My Ithaca Journal*'s diaristic entries, there are others that address a series of different issues. There are entries that meditate on growing up disenfranchised in apartheid South Africa. There are reflections on race and racism. There is the wistful rumination on my long history of being a fan of the Liverpool Football Club (LFC), which competes in the English Premier League. My history with Liverpool dates back more than half a century, as my 2007 work, *Long Distance Love: A Passion for Football*, attests. While the start of my Liverpool fandom revealed to me how my passion could connect me with a world beyond the limits the apartheid state forced on me, the end of that fandom showed me that such connections are themselves finite. It showed me that a relationship, at once chosen and the outcome of happenstance, as is often the case with so many meaningful investments, is, finally, based on people and circumstance. From an early age, then, my rooting interests have uprooted and transplanted me—not only toward the cosmopolitan but from one location to another.

A Sports Odyssey is, in part, an account of why I stopped being an LFC fan and how what happened on January 26, 2024, momentarily reactivated that fandom. What happened on that day also involves *A Sports Odyssey*'s two other principal figures: Cornell University's men's basketball coach at the time, Brian Earl, and my basketball-playing son Ezra, whom I most often address by his nickname, Nip. I am no company man and I hold elitism at arm's length, but to see a team wearing my employer's logo and my son become fans of one another propagated—propelled—my sports fandom in a new, local port of call.

Above all, however, *My Ithaca Journal* is an ode to the picaresque, a prose-poem to movement—some of it local, some of it a movement of the mind between nations, some of it rooted in the memory of being uprooted—and to the pervasive sense that all settling is but temporary and, as such, impermanent. There is a touch of the Homeric. *Journal* is about the incompleteness of the journeys I have undertaken. It is about, importantly, the feeling of loss that marks the endings of these journeys—a feeling that cannot be shaken off. *Journal*'s titular Ithaca, then, is a gift from the classical literary gods. The upstate New York college town where my family and I live, from and of which I write, Ithaca presents itself as the most appropriate location for such a series of musings about loss and impermanence. Ithaca invokes the hometown of that most famous of Homer's voyagers, Odysseus. True to the spirit of *The Odyssey*, *My Sports Odyssey* is an ode to journeys that do not end in the ways that its protagonists would prefer.

Best to admit, then, that there is something—if only vaguely—Homeric about A Sports Odyssey. *Appropriate conceptually because it, too, is informed by a spirit of restlessness—a spirit that seems more itself when unhomed; I am no Odysseus, but I do share with him a constitutive restlessness, an unease that makes it difficult to settle comfortably in the place of origin, or, in my case, both the place of origin and the place in which I now find myself.*

And appropriate because even though Ithaca, a college town in New York, is of course not the classical city of Homer's imagination, it is a town located in a region replete with classical aspiration. Within a short few hours' drive of Ithaca are towns named Utica, Syracuse, Troy, Ovid, Ulysses, Hector, Cicero, Macedon, Corinth, Rome, Romulus (but no Remus, sadly), to say nothing of Greece.

However, interspersed among the tales of wistfulness, yearning, and loss are moments of exuberance, the sheer joy and enduring human connection that only sports can offer us. Much of that pleasure derives from Cornell's 2023–24 season's men's basketball team, coached by Brian Earl. The style in which Brian's squad played; my long-standing relationship with Jon Jaques, then Brian's associate head coach and since May 2024 the head coach of the Cornell team; and the singular collection of athletes who composed that team are key figures in *A Sports Odyssey*. All of this is intensified by the closeness that Nip, my wife, Jane, and I forged with those players—the most prominent among them Zeke but also Chris, Nas, Hansen, Guy, Boothby. The ways in which those players welcomed, befriended, and, in more than one case, coached Ezra (Zeke, Guy, Nas) cemented a bond that none of us expected.

And then there is the especial aspect that Nip lends *A Sports Odyssey*. Nip is a basketball player who loves the game while refusing to allow himself to be defined by it, so that the sense of prospect simultaneously centers and exceeds basketball. Nip's love for the game is matched, I am increasingly happy to see, by his fascination with history—a fascination that has made the movie *Oppenheimer* a touchstone for how he thinks about the world and his place in it. In this way, if the number of endings—two, as we will see—are in the majority, there is about Nip the potential wonders of a tale yet to be told, a sense of athletic possibility that might yet unfold into something to behold, vistas for thinking the world as yet unknown, intellectual possibilities unknowable, as they properly should be. Regardless of how Nip's tale plays itself out, it contains within itself the promise of something, which itself is a prospect worth savoring.

The athlete who wants nothing more than to visit Hiroshima and Nagasaki.

The potential historian who asks, routinely, "Which NBA player does my game most resemble?"

On that question, Nip and I are in broad agreement: Josh Hart of the New York Knicks, a Villanova graduate.

That storied Augustinian institution would be a fine place to study history.

But, above all, *A Sports Odyssey* is about how inescapable the affective power of sport is, even when I take my distance from it or end my lifelong affiliation with LFC. And to be clear, I am not disavowing fifty-two years of fandom. I just decided that I would stop. Even with all this, in writing *A*

Sports Odyssey, I am doing nothing so much as paying tribute to precisely the phenomenon itself—Immanuel Kant's *das Ding an Sich* (the thing in itself), the affective power of sport. And, as I now realize, perhaps that power is never more manifest, never more visceral, never more emotionally overwhelming than in moments of loss.

In that moment, there is nothing to do but accede to the ruthless demand of self-confrontation. That is the moment of brutal honesty, the moment when there is nowhere to hide from yourself. That is the kind of moment, I tell myself, that maybe only a figure such as Michael Corleone can fully understand. Consider the most iconic lament in *Godfather III*: "Just when I thought I was out, they pull me back in."[3]

I stand helpless before my own inclination, indicted by it.

The best lack all conviction.

This holds true even when I want to state publicly that this is all Nip's fault, and Brian Earl's, and Jürgen Norbert Klopp's; when I want to declare that I am the victim; when I would like to claim my completely illegitimate status as the wronged party; when I am prone to denying any ambiguity on my part. *I really, really, did not want to go back in. I swear.*

I would like to say that I wrote this book against my own will and instincts. All I will admit to is that I am not yet sure as to whether this writing occurred against my own better or worse instincts.

I ask only that you, Dear Reader, believe me.

The Chronology of My Ithaca Journal.

A Sports Odyssey: My Ithaca Journal has a very specific date of origin. It also has a date of final entry, although I am always tempted to make one more addition. In the main, *My Ithaca Journal* follows a chronological timeline. From time to time, however, there are entries that are out of sequence. In these moments, *My Ithaca Journal* is disrupted through the force of history and the power of evocation. Something that happens in the *Journal*'s contemporary entries evokes a memory that belongs, more often than not, to a different time and place. There are, then, moments when a diary entry for a day in, say, February 2024 calls up a memory from a much earlier moment in, say, 1976. It is frequently the case that this rapid, jagged movement across time owes everything to stark comparison. One place, in a continent far removed, intrudes upon another. What happens in one moment brings a very different moment to mind, as if the contemporary moment and location are only fully comprehensible if they can call to life a time or a place (or both) that, while chronologically disruptive, in themselves alone have the capacity to explicate the contemporary. Or, as is more likely, the role of the earlier moment is to complicate the present and, sometimes, to throw it into sharp relief.

It is in this way that *A Sports Odyssey* constitutes a temporality that is all its own. It is, in its terms, true only to its singular chronology, thereby assigning a special narrative authority to the force of comparison. What this means is that when, say, 1976—when I was an adolescent playing football in apartheid South Africa—is invoked, it is done because it contrasts so sharply with contemporary America. This is not only a disrupted chronology, then, but a disrupted chronology that dislocates, that uproots us from one local/locale to a very different one, that throws into question one mode of apprehending how it is kids play sports by contrasting it to another where a very different ethos obtains. Conveyed here are the unexpected pleasures of incomprehension and the joys of surprise. Being able to revisit one moment in life by reflecting on a wholly different one shines a new light on both.

A Sports Odyssey will begin with one sport, English Premier League football, and with one particular event that happened on that one particular day—January 26, 2024.

It will culminate in another, Ivy League men's basketball. As such, it will span continents even as it remains resolutely local, except, as I have said, when it makes of the local a concept marked by complexity and dislocation.

Even as I was writing *My Ithaca Journal*, I knew, sadly, that it would end, as it must, in defeat. The final diary entry is that day in March 2024, when the 2023–24 Cornell University men's basketball team lost its last game of the season. Even as I hoped that they would emerge triumphant as Ivy League tournament champions on St. Patrick's Day in 2024, which they did not, I knew that this outcome would only delay the inevitable.

Cornell did not win the Ivy League tournament and so did not go on to play in the National Collegiate Athletic Association (NCAA) end-of-the-season tournament known as March Madness. It would have been a great way to end the season.

Even as I was writing on the eve of the Ivy League tournament, dubbed, almost pathetically, "Ivy Madness," I couldn't say I was brimful of optimism. That isn't my nature. But, for a moment, hope sprang eternal, even in Ithaca, no matter that there was plenty of evidence to the contrary. Suffice it to say that this Cornell team did not win its way into March Madness.

As you can surely tell by now, I grew very attached to this team, beginning with its coach, Brian Earl, Princeton University alum, class of 1999: Ivy League champ, March Madness baller, winner of a March Madness game in 1995. Look it up if you don't believe me.

Brian did not, sadly, take the 2023–24 Cornell men's team to March Madness. But he did exit splendidly, even if it was in defeat.

Cast of Characters.

The diaristic and other entries are linked, for the most part, by a recurring cast of characters that is distinctly local—that is, they all live and play their sport in Ithaca, New York, and all form part of the sport's world I inhabit there. We've already met Nip and Brian, two of the principals. In many ways, everything in *My Ithaca Journal* flows outward from Nip as a basketball player and, to a lesser extent, as a fan. Nip, who entered Ithaca High School (IHS) in September 2023, was the only freshman on the 2023–24 IHS basketball team. In fact, he was the only underclassman on the team. I'm proud of Nip for that accomplishment, but I also remind myself that that this is Ithaca, which is not exactly the kind of American college town that's likely to produce the next LeBron James or even the kind of player who will be recruited by a Division I NCAA school or, for that matter, a Division III school. A hotbed for college recruitment, Ithaca is not. I will certainly not indulge in anything so fanciful as a National Basketball Association (NBA) or Women's National Basketball Association (WNBA) player emerging from Ithaca.

As we know by now, Brian Earl's role in *My Ithaca Journal* is one of culpability. Phrased more generously, Brian can be thought of as the figure of initiation. Brian provided the spark—the key piece of information—that led to me writing *A Sports Odyssey*. In fact, it is entirely Brian Earl's fault that I wrote this book.

Isaiah "Zeke" Gray and Ezra "Nip" Farred

The orbit that is the 2023–24 Cornell men's basketball team is in many ways the centrifugal force in this book. Together with Brian Earl are the team's associate head coach, Jon Jaques, a former student of mine at Cornell University, and more than a few of the players on the 2023–24 squad. You'll meet them soon enough, but I should make special and early mention of one: Isaiah Gray, whom I've taken to calling Zeke. (Everyone else, not least of all his coaches and his teammates, refer to him as Zay.) He was a senior, a sociology major, class of 2024. For the past two years, Zeke worked with Nip on his game.

Because of Brian, Jon, and Zeke, our household has become fans of Cornell University men's basketball. Of that condition, I can only say this: it is deleterious to one's health, in the main, although there are moments of absolute joy. But mostly our household lives on tenterhooks as we watch, either live at the team's home gym, Newman Arena, or via some streaming platform, Zeke and his teammates do battle, Brian Earl's face a study in controlled intensity, refusing to give anything away. But, oh, what tempests churn within Coach Earl—tempests of a magnitude I'd rather not be privy to. But of the existence of such tempests I am convinced. Our conversations confirmed it, if not in so many words.

The Date When It Began.

January 26, 2024, proved to be quite a day—if you're me, that is.

That was the day that Jürgen Norbert Klopp, Liverpool's German manager, announced his resignation from LFC. I've supported Liverpool for fifty-two years. It would be more accurate to say that January 26, 2024, is the day that Klopp announced his decision to retire at the end of the 2023–24 season. You see, even though Klopp announced his decision on January 26, officially his tenure would run to June 30, 2024.

However, as the first diarized entry shows, Klopp's resignation was not the only important sports event to take place on that day.

It did indeed rock my world, knowing that Klopp would depart LFC. Its effect was substantial, of such an order that it drew me, for all of one week, back into my Liverpool fandom—a fandom that I had given up after more than five decades for reasons that, as you will see, continue to remain vague to me.

Three Locals.

Or, multiply local by three.

First, there is the long-distance local for me: LFC, the essence of my book *Long Distance Love*. For more than five decades, that was where, in relation to football, I lived my life.

Second, there is apartheid South Africa. This is not a local that features very often in *A Sports Odyssey*, but when it does, it tends to do so with a disruptive force. It rents things. It works dialectically. It is, explicitly, a critique of the ways in which American youth sport works.

And, finally, there is the geographical local, Ithaca, where we live, home to Cornell University, where Jane and I teach.

But that last label is, in and of itself, not exactly true, since Ithaca has a "local"—that is, central upstate New York, the Southern Tier, as the locals say—rooting that is two-dimensional. There is the truly local of my connection to the Cornell men's basketball team and Ezra's high school team. However, the local also has a downstate tendril, a professional dimension—that is, the New York Knicks.

There are moments when these locals amplify each other. There are far more moments when these locals, as I already pointed out, complicate each other.

What these three locals cannot disguise, however much as I would like them to, is the internal struggle that their coming into contact in this text sets in motion in me.

Having given up Liverpool, I have at least the pretense of never being able to love again—certainly not in the way I gave myself to LFC.

My 2023–24 engagement with the Cornell team reveals the complicated ways in which I continue, without watching or keeping abreast of LFC, to love Liverpool while also coming to understand how physical proximity can produce a new kind of bond between me as a fan and a sports team that I can root for without pledging fealty to the institution that grounds that team.

In truth, *A Sports Odyssey* stands less as a contrast between the local and the long distance and more as an expansion of what it means to affiliate locally, against self-expectation, with a sports team in a fashion unprecedented for an anti-institutional person like me. I consider myself an anti-institutional animal, so even the merest hint of institutional affiliation pains me.

As such, *A Sports Odyssey*, with its inclusion of the contradictions that only sport seems capable of provoking in a fan like me, is nothing but an attempt to give voice to how it is sport is able to resituate a fan like me in relation to a team I have historically loved (LFC), how sport makes a fan like me recall moments utterly dissonant with my current geographical and geopolitical location (apartheid South Africa), and, finally, how sport reminds a fan like me of how it can draw one into the life of a team (Cornell men's basketball team).

In *My Ithaca Journal*, I am searching for a way to chronicle how it is you learn, from scratch, to begin an attachment that, like so many such attachments and relationships, is first invited by so noble an idea as physical proximity to the team. For me, that learning has entailed watching faithfully, giving myself over to moments of rooting for this team without restraint, taking pleasure in this team in victory, and sharing with them, insofar as it is possible for a fan to share, the pain of defeat.

A *Sports Odyssey* reminds me that sport will always retain its allure for me. It will retain its allure for me because of where I am located or because of how a certain team located in a specific place—in *this* specific place—draws me toward it. Sport will always retain its allure for me, despite my protestations, despite my declaration(s) to the contrary, making of me, simultaneously, my own worst enemy and my own best friend.

If, as Shakespeare says, "conscience doth make cowards of us all,"[4] sport can make of me a man untrue to those words he swore he spoke in truth.

A Final Prefatory Word.

A Sports Odyssey: My Ithaca Journal is, at its core, my tribute to Cornell's 2023–24 men's basketball team and to their world, a world into which they allowed me a limited but immensely insightful entry. It has shown itself, my restricted access (as is proper), to be nothing less than a privilege.

I am never going to wave, as Cornell University athletic partisans do, a "Go, Big Red" banner. That would be a bridge far too far for me. I'm never going to purchase a Cornell University sweatshirt, as that is too provincial and institutional for me.

Besides, my sports soul belongs to Liverpool Football Club and Liverpool Football Club *only*.

But what a joy it has been to watch Brian Earl and his team, in person and via some streaming network or other.

This privilege has only been outdone getting to know them just a little.

The late Roger Kahn, that magnificent scribe of Jackie Robinson's Brooklyn Dodgers, remarked, when he was first assigned by *The New York Herald Tribune* to cover the Dodgers, that it was great to be with the sports writers, whom he had admired as a copy boy and now found himself, at the ripe old age of twenty-four, among.

It was great to be with the sports writers. But it was magic to be with the ball players, Kahn writes in *The Boys of Summer*, his magisterial ode to Robinson's Dodgers.[5]

Kahn's magnum opus is the first sports book I bought after arriving in the United States in August 1989. Newly ensconced in my New York apartment at 120th and Amsterdam, I took a stroll south down Broadway. Late summer, I was new to the city, and it was a good day to wander downtown. At Columbus Circle, I happened upon a street vendor who had, among his other wares, The Boys of Summer. At the princely sum of $1, how could I refuse? Molly Hite, an old friend (now sadly passed on) and former Cornell colleague, was

Brian Earl *(Courtesy of Cornell University Athletics)*

wont to say that you do not choose books; they choose you. It was a wonderful thing to have been so chosen.

Though it was not quite magic for me to hang around, from time to time, Zeke and his teammates, it was something approximating special.

So much so that when Zeke, Chris Manon, Sean Hansen, and Keller Boothby graduated, Nip, Jane, and I felt their loss. So much so that we gently chided Zeke about not saying goodbye properly.

So much so that when I speak with Brian Earl now, newly ensconced as the head basketball coach at William & Mary, I chastise him for leaving—as if I have any right.

"Stay in touch," Brian says as we hang up the phone—as if that were sufficient.

The Decision, One That Lacks a Clear Explanation.

Turns out that the final decision was, indeed, final.

There was no going back. It was irrevocable. Once made, the decision settled everything. Much as I knew this, I didn't know it—at least, I did not know it as well as I should have.

May 28, 2022: Stade de France (Paris), site of the Champions League final between Liverpool Football Club (England) and Real Madrid (Spain).

I had a ticket to the final, a rare-enough thing, courtesy of my friend Ben Carrington, a fellow LFC diehard. However, my May 27 flight from Syracuse, New York, to Kennedy Airport and then on to Paris was canceled because of bad weather up and down the Eastern seaboard. There were no flights even to Canada, a stone's throw from Syracuse. Taking the next available flight out of Syracuse would have gotten me to Paris the day after the final. Unbelieving, Ben kept urging me to find a way. It would have taken me too long to swim.

So, on May 28, around 3:00 P.M. EST, instead of taking my seat at the Stade de France, I watched, in horror, as scenes of French police attacking Liverpool fans unfolded on television.

Liverpool lost the final.

Maybe it was a good thing that my flight had been canceled. I'd have moped around Paris until my flight back to Ithaca.

I.

By May 2022, I'd been an LFC fan for more than fifty-two years.

During those five-plus decades, I'd experienced incredible highs—six Champions League triumphs, beginning with the first in May 1977, when the competition was still known, simply, as the European Cup. I'd been in the stands, with Ben, in Madrid in 2019 when we won our sixth.

I'd lived through painful defeats: Losing 0–2 to Arsenal in the final game of the 1988–89 season and with it the chance of our nineteenth First Division championship (now known as the Premier League). Losing the Football Association (FA) Cup final to Manchester United in 1977, especially painful because it was the first LFC game I ever saw live—on television, that is. Losing the 1988 FA Cup final 0–1 to Wimbledon FC, a thuggish crew unfit to lace the boots of that Liverpool team. When Wimbledon went into arbitration, I felt as if history had made me a small downpayment on the debt it owed me. Sometimes, the brutal laws of economics work to good ends.

My self-interested take on the law of supply and demand: I demand that Wimbledon go under. If only that demand had been satisfied earlier—in, say, 1987.

I'd survived terrible LFC managers. I'd gritted my teeth through other managers, enduring those not exactly to my liking.

Here, two LFC managers named Roy come easily to mind. First, there was Roy Evans (1994–98), a Liverpool native (born in Bootle), who played for the club (eleven times) and had been with LFC for twenty-eight years as a coach when he was offered the manager's job. The job never really did suit Evans. He inhabited the role as if it were too big for him (it was) and as if the opportunity had come too late in his career (it had).

If Evans seemed out of his depth, Roy Hodgson was an absolute disaster. I cannot tell you how grateful I am that Hodgson's tenure was short-lived (July 2010–January 2011). Thank God.

I admired the tactical nous of the Spaniard Rafael Benitez but found myself at odds with Rafa's deeply conservative playing style. (As a chapter in *Long Distance Love* attests, however, I remain eternally grateful to Rafa for the "Miracle of Istanbul." It was technical savvy that made possible that miracle. With his team down 0–3 at halftime, he made a couple of key adjustments, and LFC recovered to win a fifth Champions League trophy in extra time.) Liverpool has a long tradition of playing expansive, attractive football. Rafa's teams were stodgy, risk-averse, defensive; difficult to watch, they were barely tolerable to those schooled in the "Liverpool Way."

I learned, against my better judgment, maybe, to tolerate the former manager, Brendan Rodgers, although I never quite warmed to the Northern Irishman. Maybe I found him a little too glib? Or perhaps it was that he seemed to me tactically limited—as if he could only play one way, and when circumstances demanded innovation and flexibility, he was found wanting.

I shed no tears for Brendan when he was replaced by Klopp in October 2015. But neither did I wish him ill. A decent manager, Rodgers was, though not for us. And he was never of us, as Klopp showed himself to be.

II.

Part of me thinks that *the decision* is owed to the ghosts raised for me as an LFC fan by how events unfolded in Paris in 2022.

However, while what happened in Paris in 2022 does not rise to the level of the other two events that constitute this trifecta of trauma, it still shook me.

If you're a Liverpool fan of my vintage, there were triumphs aplenty. But there was also tragedy—and the trauma that emerges out of tragedy.

Heysel. Hillsborough.

So, if Paris 2022 is not exactly the third figure in an unholy trinity of death and destruction, then it certainly constituted a moment that jarred and brought specters of tragedies past but not forgotten to life.

Heysel.

First, there was Heysel, in 1984, the European Cup Final between Liverpool and Juventus of Italy. At that final, Liverpool fans were responsible for the death of Italian fans at the Heysel Stadium in Brussels. I watched that live, too. As I write in *Long Distance Love*, I will never forget what I saw unfold at Heysel. Because of the violence of the LFC fans, Liverpool (and all English clubs) were banned from European competition for five years.

Hillsborough.

Next there was Hillsborough, a stadium in the northern English city of Sheffield. Hillsborough was the (neutral) venue for the 1989 FA Cup semifinal between LFC and Nottingham Forest. At Hillsborough, on April 15, 1989, ninety-seven Liverpool fans were crushed to death because the local police refused the entreaties of dying Liverpool fans.[6] The Sheffield police refused to cut the netting that trapped the Liverpool fans, who were begging for help. That FA semifinal against Nottingham Forest was postponed. We went on to win the FA Cup that year, but what did it mean against the stark canvas that was death at Hillsborough? There are LFC players on that team (the Liverpool-born striker John Alridge comes immediately to mind) who have never recovered from that trauma. The iconic manager, Kenny Dalglish, certainly did not. Dalglish resigned in February 1991, when the trauma of Hillsborough became too much to bear.

When I watched Parisian police take their truncheons to Liverpool fans on May 28, 2022, it was not, I admit, like reliving Heysel and Hillsborough. It was a far milder manifestation of police violence, this Gallic attack on LFC fans by the local police. However, for all the difference between Heysel and Hillsborough, on the one hand, and Paris, on the other, the attack on LFC fans was too visceral for me. There was nothing I could do *not* to link them, regardless of their discreteness, regardless of the fact that the Parisian police violence in no way resembled the fatal inaction of their Sheffield counterparts.

With Paris 2022, I'd had enough of LFC-related death—or should I say deaths?

III.

That was the moment I made the decision: I could not, I would not, watch another Liverpool match.

Three traumas, spread over thirty-eight years—that's reason enough, isn't it?

The truth, however, is more obscure. I have never been able to fully explain my irrevocable decision, with the exception of a single week in January 2024, as I've admitted, to myself—or anyone else, for that matter. Fellow LFC fans with whom I've been friends for decades do not believe me. Friends who are fans of lesser footballing institutions (the likes of Arsenal, Manchester United, Leeds United, and other such inconsequential clubs) don't believe me either. And I should be clear: to support a football team other than Liverpool is to pledge fealty to a lesser footballing institution.

When I told a friend of mine who is not a football fan about my decision, he dubbed it "auto-fascism."

I've pondered his description, and I admit, although not too readily, to not being able to work out exactly what it is he means. I suspect, however, that he is onto something and that auto-fascism is a brutal form of acting against the self. Auto-fascism is the unsparing enacting of self-denial. It is a turning against the self by abjuring what it is the self loves; it is a form of violence against the self, though it doesn't exactly conform to the logic of fascism because it is the acting against the self that is without ostensible logic. It is an act of the self-withholding from itself without an adequate rationale, resolutely unyielding, inflexible, and felicitous only to the decision.

But whether partially self-comprehending or fully uncomprehending, whether auto-fascist or not, the decision was final.

No one in my family—not my wife, our sons, our daughter—believed me. Believe me, to this day, Nip expresses disappointment. Jane, I suspect, retains the notion that I'm secretly following LFC. I'm not. And I would swear to that upon my allegiance to LFC.

My friends, my family, they all assume... that there must be something. Nip and his sister, Andrea, are especially perturbed by my turn from LFC. In truth, I haven't the foggiest idea what is going through my children's heads, through the heads of longtime friends, through the minds of casual acquaintances who know me as an LFC fan. And I cannot blame any of them. After all, they've lived through decades of my very public love for Liverpool Football Club. For God's sake, I wrote a book, *Long Distance Love*, about it.

One of my oldest friends, Andrew Ross, was succinct in his disbelief: "Bullshit," Andrew said to me when he, Ezra, and I had dinner in New York City in October 2022. "Bullshit." It was hardly, I should say, a typical Andrew Ross response, this rapid, unfiltered, repeated turn to the expletive.

I cannot blame Andrew for his response. He has known me for more than thirty years, and we bonded around our shared love for LFC when we first encountered each other in September 1990 in Princeton, New Jersey.

Redoubtable Scot that he is, he shares my love of Liverpool. When we've talked since that October (2022) day, Andrew never fails to inquire. He remains as unbelieving as ever about my decision.

Other friends I didn't even tell. I still haven't told. These friends and acquaintances will be shocked when they read about my not being an LFC fan.

I console myself. Why try to explain to others what you can't explain to yourself?

IV.

I do know that with the pandemic, doubts started to creep in. Liverpool won the Premier League in a season that ended in July—July 26, 2020, to be precise—because of COVID. The season had been scheduled to end in May. For the first time in my life, I'd have to go months without football.

"Football is not a matter of life or death," the legendary Liverpool manager Bill Shankly famously remarked. "It's much more important than that." I became an LFC fan in the era of Shankly. I've quoted that phrase more times than I could possibly remember.

I've become an apostate.

The pandemic laid bare what everyone already knew. The massive global inequities in resources. The effect of this glaring disparity in wealth manifested itself during the pandemic most visibly in relation to health care (who had access and who did not), food scarcity (with millions on the brink of starvation), and education (interrupted for millions of children, many of whom would never return to the classroom, thus continuing the cycle of economic inequity). Corruption in countries across Africa, Asia, and Latin America prevented health care from being made available to the most vulnerable constituencies. COVID deniers in Florida let vaccines expire while people in Africa were dying—literally dying—for lack of access to medication being allowed to go to waste because every politician was suddenly a scientist in good standing, a Nobel laureate in waiting. The Nobel Committee was going to call any moment to award that year's prize in medicine to either the U.S. president or the governor of Florida, newly minted medical experts on a virus with which the world was entirely unfamiliar before *Coronavirus* or *COVID* was the word on everyone's lips. And every denier proclaimed themselves knowledgeable on the subject of viral immunology.

Still, I reveled in that Premier League title, and the next season, I went back to watching Liverpool.

V.

Unbeknownst to me, the pandemic may have been the beginning of the end for me.

Paris may simply have been the moment of full realization, the trauma that was not quite a trauma that sealed my fate.

A different part of me would submit its own truth. Following Liverpool has been, for me, if not a full-time occupation, then certainly a time-consuming, life-defining obsession. For fifty-two years, I spent hours every day living my Liverpool fandom—reading about it, talking to myself and friends about it. My family will attest to the several hours I spent shouting at the TV or my computer screen. They have been privy to the shouts of jubilation, they have heard my yells of utter frustration.

All this shouting, all this intense, concentrated affect—it takes its toll.

But I had years of training in this way of life. Indeed, LFC was a constant element in my life so that this, whatever this is, could not be the whole story.

Before I made the decision, I never thought myself capable of such a decision.

Such a decision.

I am still surprised by the finality of my decision.

VI.

Whatever this is . . .

I wanted to write. To write more. To think. To think more. To read. To read more. Not watching but living as much of an LFC life as I had previously lived.

But I couldn't do it in half-measures.

Maybe that's the key component of auto-fascism right there.

Obvious? So obvious I couldn't see it? Or so obvious I had to deny it?

I do know that transitioning, by going cold turkey, to a post-/non-Liverpool life freed up hours in my day.

I will always love and be loyal to Liverpool. It clearly remains, as is evident here, close to me. It remains, as it always will, an indelible, inextricable part of me.

I just don't give myself to it anymore.

What it is my work means to me, that I also cannot forswear.

Time I would have devoted to Liverpool now finds me reading or writing.

Is this how sublimation works? Or is this a kind of Calvinistic displacement, substituting one mode of pleasure-pain for another?

Writing is never easy. Thinking is work.

Watching Liverpool and following the club's goings-on was a huge time commitment.

It wasn't always easy.

I never thought of keeping abreast of the club's new signings or the potential firing or hiring of a manager as laborious.

It was a long-established part of the fabric of my life.

I had always devoted myself, equally I would say, to both.

I served two masters. Happily.

Aufhebung: *a term given to us by the philosopher G. W. F. Hegel. Most often translated as "sublate," which allows us to encounter the full range of the term's dialectical propensities to come to life.* Aufhebung: *cancel or suspend, even to abolish, while simultaneously preserving.*

LFC persists in me. In a word, Aufhebung *translates for me as the impossibility of suspending or abolishing love—my love of LFC, the indestructible truth that is my LFC fandom.*

VII.

On May 28, 2022, then, I was done.

I just didn't quite know it yet. Not in its definitiveness.

It would take a while for me to know that I was done.

Nature Abhors a Vacuum.

I. New York Mets. New York Giants.

I quit cold turkey. This was a case of auto-fascism as an act of unspeakable violence to one's (Liverpool) psyche, extreme self-denial, the complete obliteration of an essential part of one's self, the forswearing of a past integral to one's mode of being in the world—all of this, I admit, rings more than a little true. More than fifty-two years, and then you're done.

Who does such a thing?

Sublation: the impossibility of doing such a thing.

It was no matter; after Paris, I stop watching sport with any seriousness.

There was no more Formula 1, which I'd known about since the late-1960s—Jim Surtees, Phil Hill, Jack Brabham, Stirling Moss, Jackie Stewart (a driver whose iconicity carried over into the next decade), Denny Hulme—and followed closely since the mid-1970s, from the era of James Hunt, Emerson Fittipaldi, and the legendary Niki Lauda through Ayrton Senna and Alain Prost all the way to my favorite driver, Lewis Hamilton, who dominated Formula 1 in the 2010s.

I become desultory, indifferent, in the way I watch my hapless baseball team, the New York Mets. I can go for weeks sometimes without bothering to check on how badly they're doing—this after going through a season, 1993, when the Mets lost 103 games. I watched most of those losses. They remain far more memorable than that season's fifty-nine wins.

I don't like the quarterback on the National Football League (NFL) team I support, Daniel Jones,[7] so that makes it easier to watch with a caustic eye, as my New York Giants (never before has the moniker "Giants" been so rudely abused) fumble their way, once more, to a subpar record.

A more appropriate name would be the New York Lilliputians.

The Giants have not recorded double-digit victories in the regular season since they last won the Super Bowl. That's 2012; damn right, I'm counting.

Still, with the Giants, it's only seventeen games, so I can just allow myself to drift through the season. It's easy to read and maybe even write a little while watching Daniel Jones throw yet one more incomplete pass or, worse, turn the ball over. Now and then, our lad Daniel Jones puts on a bit of a show when he scrambles. I'll give "Danny Dimes" that. He can sometimes escape the pocket with alacrity.

But, pray tell, why can't a right-handed quarterback throw to his right—with any accuracy, that is?

II. A Cautionary Word about
My New York Knicks.

My New York Knicks (NYK), well, they know how to instill in their fans such a sense of hopelessness, dread, and foreboding that the guillotine might be a kinder fate.

There is, in My Ithaca Journal, *I regret to say, a New York Knicks (NYK) moment or three. And as such, a trigger warning—call it an advisory caution—is necessary. I have been a New York Knicks fan since October 1989, becoming one after I had been in the United States for barely two months. (Here's looking at you, Stu Jackson, who was then the NYK head coach.) I can only say that my recollections of the Knicks, in the time between my first succumbing to Knicks fandom and now, to be found within these pages is not to be sampled by the faint-hearted. In truth, these are reflections that are more given to that form known as the desperate screed of a long-suffering fan than it is to measured contemplation. But if being a Knicks fan for the last thirty-five years hasn't driven you mad, then I have no trouble declaring that you're either a delusional, irredeemable optimist or you're truly insane. For freaking real.*

The best lack all conviction.

Nip is also a fan of the NYK. He and I bond over our dislike of the coach, Tom Thibodeau, who drives his players so hard in the regular season that come playoff time, they've got nothing left in the tank. Gassed, they are destined to lose to teams who have a lower seed than them but are more prepared to endure a long postseason. Nip and I are incredibly fond of the now former NYK "hybrid" guard—a guard who can play both the point guard and the shooting guard position—Immanuel Quickley (IQ), traded to the Toronto Raptors in January 2024. Nip and I share a hatred—I use the term *hatred* advisedly—of Julius Randle, the most selfish, defensively averse, and unlikeable Knicks player in recent history.[8]

OK, I admit, Julius Randle is just a worse version of Carmelo Anthony.

Randle and Melo are both ball hogs. But, in Melo's defense, he could score—at least more efficiently than Randle.

The worst are full of passionate intensity.

Should I in the afterlife be condemned to Dante's ninth outer circle of hell, the case against me will be watertight. It will be no less than I deserve. Purgatory is the best I can hope for.

I condemned my son to the cruelest fate: I made him, despite my every effort, or so I say, a Knicks fan in the era of Randle.

However, with the arrival of the point guard Jalen Brunson at the start of the 2022–23 season and the acquisition of OG Anunoby from the Toronto Raptors (in exchange for, as just mentioned, IQ and the small forward RJ Barrett), Ezra and I find it less enervating and soul-destroying to watch the Knicks.

But that still leaves plenty of time unaccounted for in my day.

"About eight hours a day," my friend Jim Shepard half-mock snarled (but, in Jim's defense, it was the nicest possible mock snarl), half-laughed at me in June 2023, when I told him that I was no longer following LFC.

Jim, I should point out, is a Minnesota Vikings fan. He knows a thing or four about pain. 1970. 1973. 1974. 1977. In each of those seasons Bug Grant's Vikings lost in the Super Bowl. To, respectively: the Kansas City Chiefs, the Miami Dolphins, the Pittsburgh Steelers, and the Oakland Raiders.

III. Ezra's Team and the Cornell University Men's Basketball Team.

And so, having given up Liverpool, I commit myself to Ezra's basketball teams (which comes with its own kind of pain) and the Cornell University men's basketball team.

"You should have stuck with Liverpool," Brian remarks ruefully, a note of sympathy in his voice. As if I don't know what I've just given myself over to. Whatever else I accuse Brian of, I can't say he didn't warn me about becoming a fan of his team.

I'm no rah-rah man of the institution. In fact, it took me a while before I even knew what "rah-rah" meant, a story I'll relate shortly.

Jon Jacques (#25) *(Courtesy of Cornell University Athletics)*

IV. Nip and Zeke. Jon Jaques.

Nip has basketball ambitions, and so, in the autumn—fall—of 2022, he starts to work out with Zeke.

The last time Jane, Ezra, and I had gone to watch a Cornell men's basketball team was in the spring of 2010. We only followed that Cornell men's team because of Jon Jaques, who had been a student in my class, Sport and Literature, in the fall of 2009.

Standing 6′6″, Mr. Jaques, as I continue to call him, drained threes as that 2010 Cornell team swept all before them in the Ivy League—14-0. Mr. Jaques's team went all the way to the round of Sweet Sixteen in that year's NCAA tournament. Ivy League teams, which do not offer scholarships, are not in the habit of winning games in March Madness. The Sweet Sixteen's a historic accomplishment for an Ivy League squad, and Mr. Jaques was a key part of that team. He was co-captain, too.

V. Another Ivy League Standout.

Brian Earl and I started talking completely by accident. While I was watching a kid's summer league game in a stuffy Ithaca school gym in August 2022, Brian was trying to retrieve something that one of his sons—the oldest, Dylan, I think it was—had left courtside. Because there was a game in progress, he couldn't immediately go and find what his son had left behind. I saw him standing behind me, inclining toward to the court, and so I offered to make way for him so that he could go and get what he needed. Brian politely demurred, and we began talking.

I had no idea who he was—except I had a very good idea who he was. I knew him not as Brian Earl, the person, father of Dylan, a Liverpool fan, it turns out, who'd forgotten something that led to his dad being held captive by this strange person, or Brian Earl, head coach of Cornell University's men's basketball team.

No, I knew him in an earlier incarnation. I knew him as Brian Earl, shooting guard on the 1996 Princeton University men's basketball team.

In that guise, of course, I knew him only from a distance—that is, from watching him in the 1996 edition of the NCAA's March Madness.

I'd attended Princeton as a graduate student. I'd left Princeton in the summer of 1994 for an appointment at the University of Michigan, where "Fab Five" fever had just about broken, but the aura of those magnificent five freshmen still hung around the Ann Arbor campus. It was a thrill to watch that Fab Five team, with Chris Webber, Jimmy King, Juwan Howard, Ray Jackson, and, my favorite, Jalen Rose, with their baggy shorts, their black sneakers and socks, badass boys from Detroit (Webber and Rose), Chicago (Howard), and Texas (King, Austin; and Jackson, Plano). How that team offended the sensibilities of the NCAA establishment and the proprieties of middle-class America.

Princeton, a #13 seed, played UCLA, the #4 seed, and I watched the game from my home in Detroit, Michigan, not because I was a Princeton fan, but because I like upsets. It's the best part of March Madness, seeing lower seeds beat their more fancied opponents.

Plus, I wanted to tease my Michigan students about their loss, as the #7 seed, to #10 seed Texas. The cherry on the cake, of course, was that UCLA was the defending NCAA champion. Brian Earl was on that Pete Carril–coached team that defeated UCLA 43–41 in Indianapolis. He was an active guard, unselfish, always looking to make the pass. Under Carrill's successor, Bill Carmody, Brian would flourish as a three-point shooter. Coming off the bench in Indianapolis, Brian was a study in constant movement, leaving the job of scoring on Carril's famed "Princeton offense" to the likes of the current Princeton coach, Mitch Henderson, an Indiana native, and Sydney Johnson. Henderson and Johnson were the principal Princeton scorers.

Carril's "Princeton offense" featured a system based on his players being in constant motion. His team made backdoor cuts, attempts to get behind the defense and look for the easy basket. Some of those backdoor cuts were genuine attempts to score the ball; others were just dummy runs. Because it is impossible to tell the real from the fake when you're defending against the

Princeton offense, it has the effect of leaving opponents unsure as to whether any one backdoor cut represented a legitimate threat or if it was just a cut made to turn their heads one more time. Watching the Princeton offense can make your head spin, which has the effect, one can only imagine, of leaving opponents giddy. A key feature of the Princeton offense is multiple passes. Carril would have his team passing the ball relentlessly; the golden rule of the Princeton offense seemed to be to pass the ball until you got the shot you wanted. Brian sometimes brought the ball up the floor; at other times, he moved from one side of the floor to the other, taking defenders, who were often bewildered by this incessant flurry of movement, a Princeton player first here, then, suddenly, on the opposite side of the court. Watching that game again, I see Brian Earl, the willing backdoor cutter. In that UCLA game, it took Princeton an average of twenty-five seconds (out of a thirty-five-second clock) to shoot.

Watching Brian Earl coach Cornell, with their fast-paced game, I wonder what must be going through his head. Brian Earl, disciple of Carril and Carmody, masters of the deliberately paced game, giving his shooters free rein, taking shots early in the clock? Brian Earl, apostate? Does this churn him up inside? We'll get back to the difference between the Brian Earl–coached Cornell team and Brian's upbringing in the Princeton offense in a little while.

Add to this incessant movement the fact that Carril's team hardly bothered with offensive rebounding, which meant that Princeton, immediately after taking the shot, hustled back on defense, thereby denying UCLA the opportunity to play their favored fast-paced offense. Eating time on the clock and making a dizzying number of passes per possession, the Princeton team frustrated the UCLA players, who were unable to get out and run, causing them to commit turnovers. In short, the Princeton offense threw the defending champs off their game.

That is the Brian Earl I knew: skinny, unselfish, intense.

I watched Brian on the sidelines of Cornell games, and his Princeton intensity seems to me even more internal. Brian has taken his intensity deeper into himself, thereby privatizing what was once a very public element of his game. Disciplining his intensity, he stands with his arms folded, as though willing himself to keep everything inside, pacing deliberately, taking the same four or five steps on the same path, it seems to me. Back and forth he goes, those arms never unfolding—except when he puts his index finger to his lips; except when he is exasperated by his players; occasionally when he has a go at the refs. But mainly, you can tell how pensive Brian Earl is by how long his arms are folded.

In conversation, Brian is more relaxed, but you get the feeling that basketball is never very far from his mind.

I like talking with Brian. He has a sharp, sometimes even cutting sense of humor that can be droll. And almost every Brian Earl sentence tends to end in a smile that derives from a laugh that is equal parts sarcasm and incredulity, as if his laugh is saying, "Can you believe that?" He speaks with his face slightly upturned, his eyes doing their best to hide mischief—not always successfully. And his speech does not look askance at the odd expletive. "He's got a potty mouth on him," according to Zeke. A good man, Coach Earl. "And surely you can f-ing believe that?"

All of this is to say that I swapped my Liverpool fandom for a Brian Earl–coached team and the various teams that Ezra played on, and will play on, for at least the next three years, until he graduates high school.

Ezra wants to play college ball. Good luck to him. I'm not sure that I can take four more years after the three years of high school basketball he has left.

I barely made it through his freshman year.

The Ivies: Three Tours of Duty.

I. Irony.

Cornell, where I currently teach, is my third tour of duty in the Ivies, after graduate school stops at Columbia, and, as I've said, Princeton, so I know a little something about these institutions. And maybe I know just enough about them to not ever be overawed by them. But I can only guess as to the extent that I have been shaped by my tenure in these three institutions and how much I bear their imprint.

The irony of all of this? I did my undergraduate education at the University of the Western Cape (UWC) in South Africa. Founded in 1960 as the University College of the Western Cape, UWC is an institution that was specifically designed to cater to the apartheid state's coloured population—that is, mixed-race South Africans. Racially segregated, UWC was dubbed a "Bush College" because its standard of education was deemed inferior to that of the state's white institutions. In a designation favored by those in the disenfranchised ranks, one that sat uneasily with those related to the institution (students, faculty, staff, alumni), UWC was said to offer a "gutter education," unlike, we in the "Bush" community were made to understand, those who attended a predominantly white institution such as the University of Cape Town, where there was undoubtedly a "real" education to be had.

The Ivies will leave their mark on you, regardless, but if you graduate from out of the ranks of a gutter education and then find yourself in the hallowed halls of the Ivies, an elemental shift takes place in how it is you think your relationship to institutions of higher learning.

To begin with, there is a certain discomfiture in how it is you inhabit any space of higher education. In my book, that discomfiture is fundamentally a good thing. You sense (an intuition that endures) rather than know (as a scientific fact) that you will never quite fit, that you don't quite belong. Your sense of unease and out-of-placeness persists, because no matter how much you are in it, how long you have been in it, it will never quite be yours. However, what this discomfiture inculcates in such a conditional Ivy Leaguer as me is a singular recognition that is, to my mind, of an incalculable value: the keenest understanding of the privilege that is the opportunity to acquire tertiary education at such prestigious institutions.

It accentuates the already intense valuing of education that, in my experience, is restricted to those who retain in their thinking the memory of exclusion, whether it be their generation that was excluded or the generation(s) that came before. Such valuing owes a great deal to knowing how easily the opportunity might never have come within your grasp. It involves a sort of wistful, exacting determination to *carpe diem*.

And it comes with the recognition that you are in a position to do your work and to take joy in that recognition and in doing your work. You get to read, write, teach, think—and they pay you to do it.

It's a long way from a gutter education—an education that was never, in truth, as I have written elsewhere,[9] a gutter education.

But the good thing is that your memory of your gutter education keeps you honest.

America, land of the free to think.

Beat that.

II. Pete Carril.

The legendary Princeton men's basketball coach, Pete Carril, is said to have told his recruiters: "Don't bring me a kid with a three-car garage."

In other words, Carril wanted the kid who was hungry, that kid who was willing to work, and work hard, for the opportunity Carril was offering him. The kind of kid who would never take his place on the Princeton men's basketball team for granted. And that kid, I would hope, would hold even more dearly his right to be in a Princeton classroom.

The promise of graduating with a Princeton degree opens a new world for that kid who has no familiarity with the luxury of deciding which car to extract from the garage on any given day. And maybe, just maybe, such a kid would never forget what it was like to have never had a three-car garage.

But Princeton is also, we should acknowledge, the kind of place that instills in its graduates the inclination to acquire a house with a three-car garage.

Surely the odds are against Pete Carril finding in the son the father's hunger? The father's intimacy with socioeconomic precarity? In how many generations can the memory of such precarity endure? Is the best thing that the father can bequeath to the son not that which he now has but the making-alive for his son that which he did not have? Is it a truism to remind the father that, as a parent, it is natural to want to give his children what he did not have, thereby forgetting the value of what he as a child *did* have and, oxymoronic as it might sound, the value of what he did *not* have?

III. Education: The Question of Right.

Of course, education should be a universal right. Truth is, it all too frequently isn't. As such, there is a responsibility to that privilege, especially for someone like me, conscious as I am of a first degree obtained from a racially segregated, inferior institution.

It is recognition of privilege that has bred in me a profound impatience with those who, having been historically excluded from institutions of higher education, now take for granted that hard-won right. Those who hail from communities systematically excluded on the basis of, say, race or ethnicity, from institutions such as the Ivies and their peers—the likes of which would include such Ivy-adjacent schools as the University of Chicago, Duke, Massachusetts Institute of Technology, Northwestern, Stanford, the University of California, Berkeley—now assume their access to these institutions as a matter no longer worthy of reflection, as though it had always been so, as though it were a simply a matter of uncomplicated, unfettered right. A pox upon the house of those who teach these students who, as teachers now, have themselves lost sight of how this right was won. These students and teachers alike are unmindful of the sacrifice required to secure this access. They make too easy an equivalence between their current difficulties and the historic struggles waged by those who paved the way.

These students and teachers evoke in me an intense skepticism of their ever-greater demands for special accommodation. I can have no truck with those skilled in the art of making these ever-greater demands while only rarely—if ever—reflecting on what it is they should expect, nay, demand, from themselves during their tenure at the privileged institutions. They loudly stake their particular claim to be in these institutions but seldom, if at all, draw into question what it means to have access to such an institution. Or worse, they pay only lip service to the struggles endured, the humiliations suffered, the injustices that marred the experience of those who came before—those who, just a short historical moment ago, took up the cudgels when everything was on the line; who risked their lives, literally; who not so long ago blazed the trail, a feat never to be underestimated; who came, endured, flourished, or floundered. But upon leaving, they knew they would be forever marked by the scars of their tenure in these institutions that did everything it could to keep them out.

I take my distance from those who mobilize, with expediency, the history of exclusion of those constituencies denied entry into institutions such as the Ivies. The effects of those historic exclusions will most likely never be overcome. They caused an incalculable damage to those whom they denied access and to those who bore the burden that comes with securing first access. But those conditions in no way resemble those that obtain in our moment. Today's struggles are not those of yesteryear. It is an offense against history to suggest otherwise. Today's struggles demand at once a regard for history and a recognition of the specificities of the current conjuncture, requiring strategies that speak to what it is the moment now demands.

The question before us is thus twofold. First, how is the past to be honored? And second, how is the present to be apprehended? What responsibilities does the past demand of the present? How is the present to be engaged in a such a way that acknowledges the particularities of this moment? To repeat, how this moment is *not* that. To *know* that that means.

January 26, 2024: A Day to Remember.

At 7:15 p.m. EST, Ezra Farred, age fifteen and the only freshman on the Ithaca High School varsity basketball team, gets his first start. There are no sophomores on this team, so it's just Nip and eleven IHS juniors and seniors.

The Ithaca High School coach's habit when announcing the night's starting lineup is to write down the names on the board. This is a big day for the 6'3" Ezra, a gangly teenager who plays basketball with, in moments, a wonderfully uninhibited athleticism. It is a big day for Ezra when he sees his name on the team sheet. A basketball player with a rare disposition, Ezra is—rare not because he is some phenomenal talent. The general consensus of those who play with and coach him is that he has "potential," an attribute that fills me, his father, with some dread. After all, it requires something very particular to convert potential into accomplishment. Fulfilling potential requires a lot of hard work, discipline, and training, body and mind.

Ezra is rare among almost every one of his peers because, unlike them, his game is based on playing defense. That, he is apt to declare, is his priority when he is on the court.

In truth, ours is universally the age of offense, with the NBA leading the way, as one would expect. In today's NBA, there is three-point shooting the likes of which the game has never seen—unprecedented, all the pundits say. Here, one need only mention Steph Curry of the Golden State Warriors, who may be the greatest three-point shooter in the history of the game. This ability has garnered Steph and the Warriors four NBA titles. Today's game is replete with beautiful—and, it must be said, sometimes showy—ball handling. Here, one's thinking turns immediately to the peripatetic James Harden, on both counts. There is wonderfully efficient midrange shooting, the best exponents of which are probably Kevin Durant of the Phoenix Suns and my favorite NBA player, Kawhi Leonard of the LA Clippers. There is the physical prowess of the Milwaukee Bucks' Giannis Antetokounmpo, the "Greek Freak." There are spectacular dunks. Some of the dunks one witnesses on a nightly basis seem gravity defying. Again, one acknowledges first the "Greek Freak," but there is also the supreme athleticism of the "Ant Man," Anthony Edwards of the Minnesota Timberwolves. Here, I will allow myself an indulgence and mention Obi Toppin, formerly of the New York Knicks and now of the Indiana Pacers. Obi is no slouch when it comes to racing down the court and winding up for yet one more massive dunk. Nip and I miss the uninhibited athleticism of a freewheeling Obi dunk.

The NBA's playing style, of course, is copied by everyone, from little kids jostling in pickup games in the schoolyard, to high school athletes who have their eye on a college career and cherish dreams not only of being recruited to play Division I college ball by schools like Duke, Kentucky, UNC Chapel Hill, and so on, but of a professional career, to those college players putting in long hours in their high-intensity gyms, for whom an NBA future is the ultimate goal. Failing that, they aspire to play in the G-League (the NBA's developmental league, thus keeping alive their NBA dream), or, if the G-League is out of reach, there is always the possibility of a professional gig in, say, Europe or Australia.

Ezra is not much of a three-point shooter. To say his three-point shooting requires a lot of work would be generous.

At an Amateur Athletic Union tournament in Boston in July 2024, he first airballs a three and then, with the game on the line, nails one.

His midrange game, shooting from twelve to eighteen feet, might yet become proficient. His ball handling—what is known as "handles"—is a work in progress. He does, however, have not one but four dunks of which he can boast in his young career.

At this same tournament in Boston, Nip dunks in every one of his team's four games. So, he has at least doubled his dunk tally.

What is more, the first two of those dunks were executed on back-to-back plays. The first dunk came from a rebound taken in rhythm, followed by a few big, bounding steps, allowing him to build up speed, before he, in his words, "threw it down." The second one came from a steal, with the same result. But those dunks belong to the fourteen-year-old Ezra, when he was an eighth-grader playing against other seventh- and eighth-graders, in an athletic division known in central upstate New York as "modified."

A few days after the "dunk that was heard all around upstate New York," as Nip's brother, Alex, teases him, Ezra and I are watching the Cornell men's team practice. Ezra has sent Zeke a video of the dunk. Nip, Zeke, Nas, and Chris Manon are congratulating Ezra on his accomplishment. Over walks Mr. Jaques, who, in the most cursory fashion, inquires as to the legitimacy of this dunk. Speaking from his elevated height, Mr. Jaques wonders, with just a hint of skepticism, "Was it a regulation hoop?" As Ezra begins to stutter a response, Mr. Jaques, with a questioning smile, goes about his business. Girding that smile there is, dare I say, just the smallest trace of self-satisfaction, as if Mr. Jaques is, by puncturing—punctuating—the celebratory air, reminding Nip of just how much more work lies ahead of the newly minted eight-grade dunker. Dunking was never an integral part of Mr. Jaques's game, but at 6'6", I'm sure he threw down a few in his career.

Nip, however, may have the last word here, because his next two dunks came in back-to-back competitive games in an AAU (Amateur Athletic Union) tournament, albeit about a year after those first two dunks and before the four he flushed in Boston.

All of them were on regulation hoops.

I have yet to show any of those dunks to Mr. Jaques.

It is a version of the sport, modified, in which the contests are supposed to be competitive but also not.[10] Well, not exactly. See, this is how it works, or at least how it's supposed to work: all the players on the team are supposed to play.

For the most part, that rule holds. However, in crunch time, the coaches cannot suppress their competitive instinct, and the best players are on the court—as they should be. Modified strikes me as wildly undemocratic—the less talented kids are supposed to play for no other reason than, well, they're supposed to play. In a society as competitive as the United States, teaching seventh- and eighth-graders that simply making the team guarantees them playing time serves what purpose, exactly? What happened to earning your minutes, as coaches are apt to say? Twelve or, at most, twenty-four months hence, some of these modifiers are in for a rude awakening. They're going to get cut at the JV and varsity tryouts because no coach in his or her right mind is going to carry these modifiers just for the sake of carrying them—either they're good enough or they're not. Why delay the inevitable?

To his credit, Ezra did come close to dunking in not one but two varsity games. The first attempt failed on that rare occasion when his team—for only the second time in the 2023–24 season—was comfortably ahead, so the dunk-that-wasn't didn't affect the scoreline at all.

The second unsuccessful attempt came off a steal. According to Nip, the IHS team ended with a 2–12 record. I don't have the stomach to check the numbers. The IHS team tacked on a couple of wins in nonconference play at the end of the season. But at least one of those games was against a team that was hardly competitive. The end of the season couldn't come soon enough, for Nip or for me. Blessed relief.

If anything, Nip acquitted himself decently in his first season—disastrous for the team, hardly pleasant for him. What stood about Nip, however, is that in this, the NBA age of positionless basketball, when everyone is—or wants to be—a three-point shooter, from point guards to power forwards to seven-foot centers (or seven-foot-plus centers like Giannis's teammate Brook Lopez and Joel Embiid of the Philadelphia 76ers), Ezra's focus is stopping the opponent from scoring. He takes pride in playing defense.

Ezra's commitment to playing defense sits well with me. I've lived in the United States for thirty-five years, all of which have been purgatorial in terms of my NBA fandom. And you know the reason. I'm a New York Knicks fan.

Appropriate, then, that the high point of my fandom is the 1993–94 season, when the defense-first Knicks made it all the way to Game 7 of the NBA finals against the Houston Rockets. They lost, needless to say; and they lost in part because of the shooting guard John Starks's—you've guessed it—wayward three-point shooting. Just this past week, then Knicks coach Pat Riley finally, after thirty freaking years, publicly acknowledged his regret at not curbing Starks's profligacy. Thanks, Pat. You have no idea as to how us Knicks fans suffered as Starks threw up brick after brick, each attempt thudding off the rim with a loud reverberation, the flinty echoes of futility ringing in the ears of every Knick fan. Oh, how I still hear that cruel, cruel sound today. A loud, empty "Ping," resonating to the rafters in Houston, Texas. After Riley came clean, we'd really like John Starks to apologize to us.

Maybe now you understand why I am so full of passionate intensity.

No matter. In that fateful 1993–94 season, I came of basketball age, bitterly. But that Knicks team remains, more for ill than for good, I admit, my gold standard for how to play with intensity, unselfishness, and a bloody minded will to win. I love that team because that iteration of the Knicks was built around the defensive prowess of Charles "The Oak Man" Oakley, the late Anthony "Brick" Mason, and Patrick "The Juggernaut" Ewing.

It's true, as Roger Kahn says, that you glory with a team in victory. Kahn, however, goes on to qualify that sentiment. You may glory with a team in victory, but you fall in love with a team in defeat. Thirty years later, and I still venerate that trio of Knicks, that ethos. I was already in love with them before they lost to Houston. Just once in my lifetime, however, I'd like to savor the joy of a New York Knicks NBA championship.

Miracles we perform at once, the sages respond kindly to my desperate plea, the impossible takes a little longer.

Maybe now you understand why I lack conviction.

Still, my love for that Knicks team endures. Even now, at whatever level, whenever I see a point guard who won't pass (in today's game, this type of guard can be found at every level; these point guards learn to hog the ball early), a shooting guard who puts up a bad shot and then throws up his hands as though the gods had damned him to a lifetime of inaccuracy (but keep shooting, he will, regardless) and so excused him from defensive responsibilities, whenever I see a feckless small forward turn the ball over and then lollygag back on defense, I not only curse them (sometimes more silently than others), I wish I could conjure "Oak" up. He'd have a not-so polite word with the offender, "Oak" would, and there'd be no more of that selfishness or turning the ball over and then pretending a heinous offense had not been committed. Those Knicks, they took care of the ball. They didn't put up huge scores, mostly in the mid- to high eighties, so they protected the ball jealously. God help the player who didn't give his all on that Riley-coached Knicks team.

The current Knicks team has, as you know, one such player who could do with the "Oak" treatment: Julius Randle, who believes that "iso" (short for "isolation"—that is, going one-on-one against opponents) is the only way for him to play the game. Randle, who, after turning the ball over (which he does with regularity), will not even lollygag back on defense. Randle will just stand where he is, berate the referee, and act as though defense is a basketball task beneath a player of his caliber.

I'll give Randle his due. Reluctantly. He can post up his man. He can score.

But there is nothing of the Charles Oakley team-first mentality about Randle. And our Julius, as we know, is certainly not as gifted a scorer as Carmelo Anthony, another infernal ball hog.

Maybe now you can see why Randle evokes a visceral hatred in Ezra and me.

As a Knicks fan, how do you define a graveyard? A pass to Julius Randle. It's where passes go to die.

Oh, how I miss you, "Brick," "Oak," and "The Juggernaut," how I wish you'd come back and take Randle to task.

Rebounds, blocking shots—these are what motivate Ezra. Ezra rebounds, I am apt to say, like someone's about to steal his Chicken McNuggets, a staple of Ezra's diet, along with pizza, saag paneer, gyoza dumplings, and Manchego cheese (mild or medium, if you please). A diet determinedly international is the best that can be said of Nip's food preferences.

Blocking an opponent's shot is what Nip is apt to recall with a devilish glint in his eye and a rather unsettling joy in his voice. I suspect that blocking a shot, especially with his weaker left hand, is more satisfying for Ezra than even an end-to-end dunk.

In one of the final IHS games, against Horseheads High School, February 8, 2024, Nip doesn't get much time—in total, less than four minutes, in fact. But, on the first play in which he is in the game, he blocks a shot. With his left hand. Even from where I'm sitting, on the far side of the floor, I sense the steely look in Ezra's eye. He doesn't flex his muscles, but he might as well have.

Of course, IHS loses. Again. Two more losses to go. Season ends on February 15, 2024.

It was a banner day for Ezra—his first start.

But, this landmark day in Ezra's young career isn't, as you already know, the only thing on my mind.

7:30 p.m., January 26, 2024: Ezra's Starting.

"Ezra's starting," I text Zeke. As their basketball schedules permit, Zeke and Ezra work out once or twice a week.

Zeke, always a man with a smart quip at the ready, responds, "They like the dog in him."

Ezra and Zeke have been working together for almost two years, and Zeke likes how hard Ezra practices and plays, although he calls Ezra out from time to time when his protégé's concentration flags. And there are enough of those moments for Zeke to keep Ezra on his toes.

True to form, IHS succumbs to defeat once again. And once again, the margin of victory is somewhere on the order of thirty points.

With a current record of 2–11, this HIS team has lost by somewhere in the region of three hundred or so points.

I doubt they've scored more than 250 points in total.

These statistics make for grim reading.

At least they're consistent: the same result, game after game, a wrinkle here, a minor adjustment there, but largely the same starting lineup, game after game. It's hard not to find comic relief in Einstein's definition of insanity.

January 27, 2024: Charles Oakley.

4:45 P.M.: "He's Charles Oakley," Zeke teases Ezra, or "E," as he and Nas call Ezra, after we'd gone to watch Cornell University beat Princeton University, convincingly, the next day, on Cornell's home floor.
　Zeke is 6′3″. He's got the physique of a bull mastiff—strong legs, a barrel chest, and powerfully muscled shoulders.
　When Zeke attacks the basket, his face is a study in controlled aggression and intensity. When he is driving for a layup, he presents a formidable challenge to the opponent—or opponents—guarding him.
　Facing Zeke in game mode is like confronting the most solidly constructed bowling ball steaming downhill at you, gathering pace. I worry for the physical safety of the opposing players.
　It goes without saying that Zeke always draws one of the toughest defensive assignments for the Cornell team. Zeke takes pride in this. I'm pretty sure he wouldn't want it any other way. In this regard, as in a few others, Zeke and Nip are alike. They're both defense-first players.
　Nip couldn't have had a better coach these last two years.
　Today, against Princeton, Zeke is injured (a bone bruise in his left foot), so he didn't play in the win. But he's pumped up with the victory, so he's happy to joke around with Ezra.
　I'm in the bathroom at halftime with Cornell up by nineteen. I hear two Cornell students, drying their hands, complain: "Our best player"—they're referring to Zeke—"why isn't he playing?"

"He's got a bone bruise," I interject. Neither of these two Cornell students look like they've played a single competitive game in anything in their bespectacled lives. I doubt they'd survive a robust game of tiddlywinks. No matter. They feel free to pronounce on Zeke's absence as though it were a personal offense.

"Yeah," one of them shoots back, "he could save that for Dartmouth. We need him today."

Fair enough. Dartmouth is not Princeton.

Why can't Zeke just up his pain threshold level?

Really, Zeke, why not?

In late January 2024, Princeton, Yale, and Cornell sit atop the Ivy standings, each boasting perfect 3-0 records. By the end of the day, that will only hold true for Cornell and Yale. Dartmouth is a dismal 1-3.

But, I hasten to add, you underestimate Dartmouth at your peril.

They breed 'em tough up in Hanover, New Hampshire.

Intra-Ivy Envy. Or, Which of These Five Schools Is More Insecure about Its Ivy Status than Its Peers? Or, Only in America.

As Hisham Matar writes in his memoir, *The Return: Fathers, Sons, and the Land in Between*, "Anxiety is a shameful business."[11]

If Cornell is held in lower esteem by the Big Three (Harvard, Princeton, and Yale) in the Ivy League, the Big Red can at least mount a good political defense.

Cornell is the only hybrid institution in the Ivy League. That is, it has both a private and a public "side." The private side is what you'd expect (College of Arts and Sciences, College of Engineering, College of Architecture, and so on), and it attracts the kind of aspirational students you'd expect (kids who want to go to med school, law school, business school, grad school, to which we might add grad school in engineering; we can also throw into the mix those dwindling numbers of English and History majors, together with a small constituency of kids committed to social justice). The public side includes the College of Agriculture and Life Sciences, Industrial and Labor Relations (ILR), and so on. These students have a professional career in mind; indeed, in addition to becoming, say, a public rights advocate, some of the ILR graduates will go to law school, after which they anticipate a lucrative career in a big corporation. Don't be fooled by the ILR moniker, which suggests a certain commitment to defending the interests of the workers. Some ILR grads will do precisely that, while others will in fact work against workers' interests. A Cornell ILR degree is a ticket into the world of big business, and there's nothing capital dislikes more than paying the workers their fair share. Learn about industrial relations in order to thwart the ambitions of labor; become a lawyer so as to know how best to maximize worker exploitation.

A sign in Ives Hall proudly announces: one in two Fortune Five Hundred Companies have an ILR graduate on their board.

How better to put one over on the workers than to learn all about the relations that govern their conditions of labor?

You have to give late capitalism its due: it is ubiquitous, it is unrelenting, and it will leave no (institutional) stone unturned.

It is in the very air I breathe every Tuesday and Thursday when I teach in Ives Hall.

What I like about Cornell's hybrid nature is that it affords kids from all over, but especially those from upstate New York, whose interests tend toward the pragmatic, the opportunity to graduate with an Ivy League degree. Furthermore, students can take classes in both the public and the private, thereby minimizing the distinction between the two sides of the institution. Any Cornell class can, therefore, include both students from, say, a hardscrabble neighborhood in Canandaigua—upstate New York, just east of Rochester—and from, say, Manhattan. Kids who graduated from a public high school in Albany, New York, rub shoulders with kids from exclusive New England prep schools.

No other Ivy has this private-public mix. Such hybridity would certainly not be tolerated at Harvard, Princeton, and Yale. In fact, the Princeton Tigers have no professional schools—graduate schools, yes, but no law, medical, or business schools. (No "Juco"—Junior College—transfers on the Princeton team. The Princeton rule is absolute: if you have an undergraduate degree from any other institution, to say nothing about so lowly an accomplishment as an associate's degree from a community college, you can't get an undergraduate degree from Princeton. Cornell accepts transfer students. An associate's degree is not an insurmountable obstacle to those considering Ithaca as an option. There are a couple of Jucos on the Cornell team. One of them, Max Watson, saw a lot of playing time last season.)

In fact, during my time at Princeton, the Tiger undergraduates would taunt the Ivy League teams from the University of Pennsylvania with a decidedly undemocratic chant: "Penn State, Penn State," the cry would go up. That cry echoed from the student section of Jadwin Gym.

Penn State is a public university, and a very good one, at that, with its main campus in State College. My wife used to teach there before coming to Cornell, and two of my colleagues who number among my chief interlocutors are on faculty at The Pennsylvania State University, although one of them, I am sad to say, has since retired.

The rich kid Duke University basketball fans, in their famed Cameron Arena, have their own version of this chant. When the Duke team is losing to the neighboring North Carolina State University team, the cry would go up from the Dukies: "It's alright, it's OK, you're going to work for us someday."

I'm sure there are other such rich kid chants at privileged institutions, as the next entry will attest.

Brian Earl's elder brother, Dan Earl, played at Penn State (1993–99).

I wonder how those chants that echoed around Jadwin resonated with Brian. A strange animal is this world of the Ivies, where (intra-ruling) class warfare takes the form of deliberately misrecognizing the private for the public; where misnaming your opponent "Penn State" is the kind of taunt that constitutes the gravest insult. This, one supposes, is how the American elite—and, of course, the global elite who fill the ranks of the Ivy schools—configures class distinctions. This is how one separates the Ivy wheat from the Ivy chaff.

But Ivy chaff is a chaff like no other.

It may be that it is only at the very highest echelons and among the very lowest denizens of society that the distinction in status is most fine-grained. Not all Ivies are equal.

In *The Return*, Hisham Matar castigates himself for being anxious about his inability to be without his cell phone after the revolution in Libya. Such an anxiety seems fully explicable to me and not shameful at all. But intra-Ivy envy—is there an anxiety more shameful than that?

In the scheme of things as described in *The Return*, where the devastation of a society by Muammar Qaddafi hangs heavily over Matar on his return to Libya, it is doubtful, I'd say.

Class Warfare in the "Little Ivies."

When I served, as I am apt to recall with great fondness, as the JV coach of the Williams College football team in the autumn of 1999, we played a game against North Adams State. (North Adams now goes by a much grander name: Massachusetts College of Liberal Arts.) North Adams is the next town over from Williamstown, Massachusetts, and it is one of those fallen-on-hard-economic-times postindustrial communities.[12] Though not as derelict as, say, Utica, New York, or as depressing as, say, 1970s Cleveland, Ohio ("The Mistake by the Lake"), North Adams possesses none of the small college town New England charm of Williamstown.

Plus, it's a working-class community, and many of the folks who live there are employed in administrative and maintenance positions at Williams College.[13]

The North Adams State team was a rugged but not unskilled bunch. We won. There was some edge to the contest. After all, these two schools are neighbors; nothing but a mile or two separates them from each other. When I lived in Williamstown, the only place to get groceries—Stop & Shop—was in North Adams.

To be clear, I've got nothing against smack talk on the basketball court or on the football pitch.

As the match was in progress, however, I heard a retort that took me aback.

"You're going to work for us," a Williams player said, and not in the heat of battle. It was just a sideline quip from a Williams player who didn't like something a North Adams player did, a throwaway line. No one else raised an eyebrow.

Kid from a working-class background that I am, my political sympathies were aroused.

Growing up in a working-class township (the equivalent of a U.S. project) in Cape Town, South Africa, I may teach at Williams, but I'm too much the product of my disenfranchised past to be party to such ruling-class disdain.

In my career, I played on working-class clubs against plenty of middle-class teams, where I did my fair share of jawing. I know class ressentiment. I came by mine honestly. I know its sting. I know just how it can fuel a player. It certainly got my motor all revved up in those days of yore. But this disregard for an opponent just because they're students at a much less well-funded public institution—this is new to me. It strikes me as beyond the pale.

Mercifully, the Williams culprit is not on my JV team. But, the next day at practice, I make it clear that such behavior is verboten, for my players, anyway, and certainly not when I'm in earshot.

Williams, I should point out, is one of those elite New England colleges (along with, among others, Williams's historical rival, Amherst College, and Bowdoin College in Maine) that make up a collection of liberal arts schools known as the "Little Ivies."

Or, as one of my Williams students described it to me, and not fully in jest, "We're all Harvard rejects." More than twenty-five years later, I'm not sure if his self-designation should have saddened me or if I was too lacking in a patrician New England sensibility to appreciate his self-deprecation—or was it irony?

I can see him still, that student: tallish, carefully attired in regulation khakis and a button-down shirt, hair neatly cut, bespectacled. He was a serious student.

I had no reason not to take this Williams student at his non-ironic word. It seemed to me too well thought, that self-description, for me to dismiss, even if it was a throwaway line. The student may have forgotten that he made that remark to me, but it clearly left a lasting impression.

Teaching at Williams College was my pedagogical nirvana; it involved two semesters, each twelve weeks long, teaching smart and sometimes even brilliant students (a second-semester freshman producing a Lacanian critique, with sharp insights, remains with me to this day—here's looking at you, Ms. Sheppe, New Hampshire native), intensely committed and wonderfully prepared. Given all of this, why would "Little Ivy" students want to indulge in such self-denigration?[14]

Dartmouth, Again, Briefly.
But Not for the Last Time.

As I said earlier, in 1999, I coached the Williams College JV football (soccer) team. Williams is a Division III school. Our biggest victory, by some measure, was against Division I Dartmouth, up in faraway Hanover, New Hampshire. We won 3-0. From the kickoff, we strung together twenty-two passes. I counted them. And then I recounted them, reliving each one. Our twenty-two passes resulted in our first goal before Dartmouth had even touched the ball.

Effectively, the manner of our opening goal put an end to the contest.

Our two standout players of that season, the erudite central midfielder, "Dough Boy," and our prolific striker, Dylan Engel, played their best football that day.

As we were up 3-0 in twenty minutes, I instructed my players not to score again. And I gave our second stringers plenty of time.

Twenty-five years later, I watch a high school JV basketball coach put his best player back in with less than three minutes left, just so that his team—already up by forty or fifty—could get the score to a hundred. Said best player obliges by draining a three. Said player then celebrates his accomplishment. His teammates, one and all, join in the festivities.

It is customary, when entering a gym at an American school, to see, on a notice, something along these lines:
Let the players play.
Let the coaches coach.
Let the refs ref.
Let the spectators cheer. (Or some such inanity.)

We encourage good sportspersonship. (On which, more later.)
What could be more sporting than humiliating an opponent?

The opposing coach, seeing his opposing number run up the score, takes umbrage, and rightly so. The winning coach is unrepentant.

Words, of the unpleasant variety, are exchanged between the coaches at the final whistle.

You know whose side I'm on.

It isn't cricket, CLR James, cricket scribe extraordinaire, would have admonished the winning coach.

It isn't done. Do not humiliate an opponent.

Intra-Ivy Fraternal Tensions, Continued.

Misnaming your Ivy opponent and flaunting your class superiority—what greater insult could there be?

Outside of the Big Three, Harvard, Princeton, and Yale, every other Ivy suffers from its own particular strand of inferiority. *Having graduated from one of the Big Three, I have to say that I am in no way intellectually overimpressed by Harvard, Princeton, or Yale. They can seem to me precisely the place where thinking is abjured. As if the letterhead were its own accomplishment. As if the letterhead were, in and of itself, enough. As if these institutions, and those like them, were precisely the kind of places where minds go to die.*

Each has their own unique complex, one that locates them as lower on the Ivy totem pole—Brown, Columbia, Cornell, Dartmouth, and UPenn—where they jostle, I'm imagining, for positions four and five. Who wants to be ranked eight out of eight?

A friend of mine who did his first year of undergraduate study at UPenn tells me that during his time there, the students would exchange notes as to which Ivy had rejected them. (Yale, in his case, he recounts with a smile. And not a rueful one. Bless him.) David went back to Texas and got his degree from the University of Texas at Austin.

Columbia, where I did my MA, at least has the great benefit of location—Morningside Heights, the Upper West Side of New York City.

Let the other Ivies say what they want, but Columbia has the city—simply *the city*; no need for capitalization. After all, what other city could possibly lay claim to being *the city*? Not Boston. Not Philly. Who cares about

Ivy rankings when you can wake up overlooking the Hudson to the west, Harlem to the north, and Central Park and the Metropolitan Museum within easy reach to the east. South of you, there's downtown—Lincoln Center, Times Square, Soho, the Village . . .

Cornell may be the only hybrid Ivy, but at least the school is not located in what I like to call the upper reaches of northern Appalachia. That is, Cornell students call Ithaca home, and Ithaca is not, mercifully, Hanover, where Dartmouth finds itself. Hanover is not quite the archetypal Appalachian world of Thomas Wolfe's *Look Homeward, Angel*, but lots of folks up that way know each other, and when I say know each other, I mean that they know each other well—really well.

Location, location, location: that's Columbia's selling point; it's *the urban Ivy*. Sorry, Boston, Philly, and Providence.

Cornell students are sensitive about their hybrid status. In class, I take a certain delight in teasing them about it. "I went to a *real* Ivy," I say.

And then there comes that moment during the 2023 home game against Dartmouth. In a contest that is closer than it should be, Cornell makes a run, the final push that will put Dartmouth away and secure the victory.

An especially enthusiastic Cornell student, directing his comments pointedly at the visiting Dartmouth fans, gives public voice to this peculiar form of anxiety known as intra-Ivy envy. His outburst vocalizes insecurity: "So the hybrid Ivy's beating the *real* Ivy," he exclaims, maybe a little too exuberantly. If you have a public dimension to your Ivy League institution, you've got a chip on your shoulder the size of one of those boulders that majestically flank one of Ithaca's many gorgeous gorges. "Ithaca is gorges," the local bumper stickers announce.

The visiting Dartmouth fans, clad in green, look the other way. I wonder if they're not chuckling on the inside, seeing the Cornell psychosis laid bare, loudly, for everyone in the arena to hear, thinking, perhaps, "Yes, we're losing, but at least we're a real Ivy."

Zeke should have scheduled his bone bruise for a lesser Ivy.

February 2, 2024.

The folks in Hanover must have heard those two cocky Cornell undergraduates in the bathroom at halftime at Newman Arena. Cornell starts off against Dartmouth like a house on fire. With just over ten minutes left in the first half, Cornell is up 19–0. Dartmouth can't buy a bucket. Good shots drop halfway down the cylinder, only to reject their downward trajectory, as if the laws of physics don't apply to Dartmouth shots. Layups rim out. In this contest of Ivy colors, the "Big Green" of Dartmouth looks hapless against their "Big Red" opponents.

For the next thirty minutes, it's a different story.

Cornell leads 27–21 at halftime.

Dartmouth comes out strong in the second stanza and takes the lead—by as many as six or eight.

At this point in the contest, Dartmouth has outscored Cornell 53–29.

But Cornell claws its way back in front in the final two minutes.

Late in the game, Cornell's backup center, Guy Ragland Jr., strokes a clutch three, Zeke makes two free throws, Manon makes one out of two at the stripe, and Nas seals the victory with less than a minute left as he drives the lane and, off balance, puts up a perfect floater.

I call Nas the next morning and accuse him, with absolute justification, of taking years off my life.

He chuckles. "Mine too."

About his floater, I remark: "You were off-balance, falling backward."

Nazier "Nas" Williams (*Courtesy of Cornell University Athletics*)

Nas, being Nas, has the perfect response: "That's when I'm most on-balance."

You gotta love the kid. The kid and his team drive you nuts.

The final score is 56–53. Cornell edges Dartmouth in a squeaker.

Through it all, as is characteristic of him, Brian Earl keeps his cool, appearing as poised as a coach can be when their team's blown a nineteen-point lead. I can't imagine, however, that it will be a fun ride from Hanover to Cambridge, Massachusetts.

Hopefully, this is a lesson learned and they come out strong against Harvard tomorrow night and sustain their intensity for forty minutes.

This Dartmouth win cannot be good for anybody's health, starting with mine.

January 27, 2024.

Instead of planning his injury more to the liking of his fellow Cornellians, Zeke had to get hurt against Brown University, another not-so-highly regarded Ivy.

That win against Brown, on January 20 in Providence, Rhode Island, was ugly, and it could easily have gone the home team's way.

When Cornell visits, Brown has only one win, which seems hard to believe, given how they pushed the Big Red all the way.

Sometimes there's truth to coaching truisms, especially the one about there being "no easy games in our conference." That's a line that Brian Earl likes to use.

Brown sent Cornell a warning. We'll see if it's heeded, especially when Cornell plays Brown the night after the Yale game at Newman Arena. The focus that weekend, which is Senior Night, will surely be on the Friday night game against Yale. Brown could be a banana skin.

It would be painful to slip up against a team that has thus far mustered one Ivy League victory.

What can Brown do to you? They can beat you on Senior Night.

A Colored Ivy. Penn, Again.

It is too easy to make fun of Brown. After all, it's a color, and, with all due respect to the color brown, there's nothing very sexy about it; in fact, the color, left to the imagination of hyped-up Ivy late-adolescents (or, in truth, any adolescent, of any age), is sure to invite scorn about certain bodily functions. The worst thing about the color brown is that it's not black. For these reasons alone, Brown should not be the name of an Ivy League school.

But there are other reasons, such as the fact that Brown University has a historic connection to the slave trade.[15] Then again, what prestigious institution in the United States doesn't? Princeton, Williams, Georgetown, the College of William & Mary—the list is a long one. After all, how do you think the Wharton family, engaged as they were in the iron industry, made their fortune? Named after John Brown's nephew, Nicholas Brown Jr., Brown University as an institution represents an only-in-America historical paradox. John Brown's commitment to the revolution was countered by the "Brown brothers'" involvement in the slave trade.[16] Nicholas Brown gave his name to an institution that had gone by a rather nondescript but not unusual for that period in U.S. history moniker, the College of Rhode Island, similar to Princeton's first incarnation, the College of New Jersey. Harpers Ferry was, so to speak, a long way from the "merchants in Providence and Newport [who] dominated the American arm of the African slave trade."[17]

To its credit, under the leadership of its first African American president, Ruth Simmons, also the first African American president of an Ivy League institution, a committee was set up to investigate Brown University's implication in the slave trade. The University Steering Committee on Slavery and Justice was established in 2003 and issued the "Report of the Brown University Steering Committee on Slavery and Justice" in 2006. The Brown Report set off shockwaves in U.S. higher education, initiating a series of inquiries that revealed the often-foundational relationship between the most prestigious U.S. institutions and the slave economy.

The pragmatist Emerson, no man of action, admired John Brown.

I wonder if the rebellious spirit of John Brown looked upon with approval Simmons's appointment and political audacity, her determination to unconceal the ugly truth of Brown University and slavery—a truth that must, not in 2003 but long before, surely have been widely known, if not publicly acknowledged.

Ruth Simmons is what the spirit of (John) Brown can do for you.

And just in case you're wondering, the answer is *no*. It is a question Jane and I get from time to time. So, again, Ezra is not named after Mr. Cornell. He owes his name to a cricketer from Barbados, the fast bowler Ezra Moseley. Slim, athletic, and wicked quick with an easy bowling motion was the late Ezra Moseley (January 5, 1958–February 6, 2021). Mosely died in his native Barbados; he was killed by a motorist when he was out cycling on a day that also happened to be Bob Marley's birthday. Ezra., furthermore, shares a birthday with the Barbados native, Sir Garfield Sobers, the greatest cricketing all-rounder of all time. (In cricket, a player who can bat *and* bowl with equal proficiency is known as an all-rounder. It is more common for cricketers to be better at batting or bowling.)

Penn, in the version I glean from my students, is every bright young high school student's "safety school." The logic goes something like this: it's the Ivy you apply to because you know you're good enough to get into, but you're pretty sure that the Big Three is too much of a stretch. So, if, say, Cornell or Brown or Dartmouth reject you, well, at least you graduate with an Ivy degree. And there's something unapologetically incorporative, unabashedly colonialist, and, unquestionably, geographically expansive about being named after an entire commonwealth.

The kind of student who has their heart set on the Ivies is probably too much of an urban animal to countenance Williams (population seven thousand, of whom two thousand were students, when I lived and taught there) or Amherst, and maybe Maine's just too cold, so that rules out Bowdoin, and with that goes the application to the "Little Ivies."

Off to Philadelphia you go, you bright young thing.

Zeke, In Profile.

In purely statistical terms, Zeke is not Cornell's best player. In this, the 2023–24 season, that honor belongs to Chris Manon, a maniacally talented guard.

Chris can shoot. He can drive, sometimes with sublime skill. When he dunks, he rises with effortless grace. He plays tough defense. And Chris Manon is always smiling. It's hard not to love Chris. He is charismatic. And sometimes he just drives the Cornell coaches nuts, as he is all too capable of making some boneheaded decisions. This season, however, Chris is keeping, as far as possible for him, his emotions in check, and he may be the best player in the Ivy League, after Yale's standout floor general Bez Mbeng, Yale coach James Jones's coach on the floor.

Chris plays defense, as he does everything else, with a smile. This is not so for Zeke.

Zeke, arms akimbo, forming a V (as though he were a bodybuilder flexing his muscles), feet at once firmly planted on the court and poised for movement, menaces his opponents on defense. Defense is Zeke's calling card.

A kid from Brooklyn, New York, Zeke knows his basketball history. Guy Ragland does too—he's sort of Rain Man-ish. Without taking a moment, he can tell you in exactly what year his New England Patriots won the Super Bowl. He can tell you, without blinking, whether Aaron Hernandez won one or two Super Bowl rings.

So, when Zeke evokes "Oak," it brings a smile to my face. "Oak," as I like to remind Nip, was a tower of strength on both the offensive and defensive boards for the Knicks.

Ezra's no "Oak," but it's nice of Zeke to say so. (For one, my fifteen-year-old son is at least seventy pounds shy of "Oak" at his Knicks fighting peak and a good five inches shorter.)

If anything, Zeke—allowing for the height differential with Oakley—is more like "Oak" in his rugged, intelligent style of play.

Driven to win, Zeke is.

January 27, 2024: Beating Princeton.

In the corresponding fixture in the 2022–23 Ivy League season, Princeton inflicted a painful defeat on Cornell at Newman Arena.

A missed Cornell layup here (Sean Hansen), a turnover there, and key shots late in the game by Princeton swung that 2023 contest Princeton's way.

Today's matchup is a different story.

I always wonder what is going through Brian Earl's head when he goes up against Princeton—especially at Jadwin, especially going up against his old teammate Mitch Henderson.

Tonight, Brian Earl has his team ready. Cornell comes out focused. It is a complete performance.

Chris Manon is on his game, the hardworking power forward/center Sean Hansen commands the boards, the mercurial, feisty, and wonderfully talented point guard Nas Williams is playing under control. It is a thing to savor, Nas playing under control. You get to see how good he really can be.

I think of Nas as a *force de vie*, a vital life force. Nas is entirely lacking in pretense. He has the demeanor of a twelve-year-old. He just oozes life. He is confident, puckish, mischievous. Nas has the smile of an eight-year-old *voyou*; he is pure lovable rogue. He also has the diet of an eight-year-old.

January 31, 2024.

Nas and the freshman guard Jacob Beccles come to watch Ezra play. Its IHS's Senior Night, so Ezra doesn't play much. In fact, he only gets four and a half minutes in the final quarter. Nas and Beccles, who has been given the nickname "Jiggles" by Guy Ragland, come up and join me in the stands, each holding two or three packets of candy and a can of soda. It is all I can do to stop myself from saying something. These are Division I athletes who would the next day (February 1) be embarking on a five-and-a-half-hour bus ride to Hanover. And this is their diet—candy and soda that they've purchased from a high school concession stand.

IHS perform with their usual ineptitude. Nip's school is playing Johnson City, and the Johnson City shooting guard, Z. Griffin (#20), scores fifty-two points in three quarters. *Three quarters.* As soon as Griffin gets his final bucket, their coach sits him. Johnson City coasts to a 101–47 victory.

Nas and Beccles thrill to the Griffin performance, which leads to them recalling their high school stats.

I like watching IHS games with Nas and Beccles. I like watching with them because they, apart from being there to watch Ezra, have no skin in the game. This allows them to appreciate and criticize both teams' performance, and they feel absolutely free to acknowledge good play—individual and collective—from IHS's opponents. When they're not there, I know that I am making myself conspicuous by applauding when the other team does something well.

Remember that notice at the entrance to the gym? Remember the part where it says "be a good sport"? Well, they really don't mean it. What they *mean is be a partisan. Only root for your team. Do not acknowledge it when the opposing team does something well. Tribalism distilled to its small town essence. Not at all in the spirit of being a good sport. Petty.*

In recent years, Manchester City and Liverpool have established themselves as the top two teams in the English Premier League. I always want Liverpool to beat them. But City's talisman, Kevin De Bruyne, is a joy to behold, as is Bernardo Silva. *And I feel free to say so, even if it is only to myself. In my basement.*

A shooting guard at Constitution High School in Philadelphia, Beccles tallied 1,460 points, averaging 25.4 at Constitution before spending a year at Lawrenceville Prep, where his average increased to 27. Nas, his smile as wide as ever, tells us that he needed 29 points in his final high school game for 1,000 but could only manage 27.

Because of Nas, I now have the number 998 drilled into my head. It is a number I will from now on associate exclusively with Nas.

January 27, 2024.

Zeke's replacement in the starting lineup, the Californian AK Okereke, a walk-on sophomore, is a study in discipline and unselfishness. Unselfishness to a fault—that's what AK's all about. He does all the little things. He is a tough defender, he is always looking to pass; he'll do whatever it takes, as coaches like to say, to secure the win. Cooper Noard, the smooth-stroking shooting guard from Illinois, strikes me as a finesse player who, as is characteristic of this Brian Earl team, always puts in an honest shift. It doesn't matter if Cooper's number is called on offense or not. Noard plays solid defense, he is adept at finding the open man, and he takes the right shot at the right time.

Off the bench, the senior from Plano, Texas, Keller Boothby, moves smartly without the ball, taking up positions at the top of the key. Are Boothby's movement and his positioning, which were not part of his game last season, I wonder, causing confusion on a Princeton defense that has him pegged (solely) as a deadly three-point shooter from the wing?

Keller "Smooth Operator" Boothby, I always marvel, has an NBA shot. In moments, it can seem sublime—beautiful arc, textbook form. The "Smooth Operator" is supremely efficient; there is no wasted motion.

Take that, Sade.

Keller Boothby *(Courtesy of Cornell University Athletics)*

"Over-Rated."

The Princeton guard, Xaivian Lee, comes into the game against Cornell with a lot of hype. Rumor has it that there have been NBA scouts watching him—at least, that's the word on social media, so I'm told. I don't do social media, so I take the Cornell fans at their word.

The Cornell student section, ever alert to this, gets on Lee from the start.

Every time Lee touches the ball, the Cornell students break out into a chant, in fearsome unison: "Over-rated! Over-rated!"

It's difficult not to agree with them.

Lee's nowhere the player that Chris Manon is.

I suspect there's something else going on here with Lee.

Perhaps it's the lingering Jeremy Lin effect.

Or, the Jeremy Lin aftereffect.

Lin played at Harvard. He wasn't drafted and spent half a season actually playing, rather than just riding the bench, for the New York Knicks. He had a fantastic run for the Knicks and hit a few game-winning shots.

The Knicks, to their credit, made one of their few smart personnel decisions.

They did *not* re-sign Lin at the end of that one season (2011–12).

Lin signed for the Houston Rockets, instead, where he was, as expected, a bust. He drifted around the NBA after that—the Los Angeles Lakers, Charlotte Hornets, Brooklyn Nets, and Toronto Raptors, where he won an NBA championship, but as a bench warmer.

NBA scouts were embarrassed at having missed Lee during that freak streak with the Knicks.

Kobe Bryant made a big noise about it.

Those scouts should not have worried. There was no need to have second-guessed themselves. Their judgment was sound all along.

My sense is that the NBA scouting community doesn't want to be caught with its pants down again—hence, the Lee hype.

Cornell destroyed him.

However, I will say this. Lee fights really hard through screens to get open. And when he does get open, he is very likely to make you pay with his shooting, especially from long range. And, unlike Chris, Lee does tend to play under control. With Chris, sometimes you don't know what you're going to get.

Lee, however, is miles behind Chris Manon in terms of talent and sheer athleticism.

As a matter of fact, Lee's hardly a match for Nas.

Again, however, as a point guard, Lee plays under control. Nas, sometimes not so much. Nas can sometimes force plays. Lee, like every other player, sometimes makes bad decisions, but he tends to make fewer bad decisions than Nas.

So enough with this silly Lee hoopla, already.

"Over-freaking-rated!"

11:25 a.m., January 30, 2024.

In spring 2024, I teach from 11:40 a.m. to 12:55 p.m. in Ives Hall. This is my first time teaching in Ives, a building on Cornell's main campus, about a mile from where my department is situated. As I stand outside Ives 219, waiting for the class that meets there before mine to empty out, along comes Keller Boothby. Redheaded and with a full beard, he towers over me. I've always taken him to be a quiet lad, but Ives Hall is part of where Boothby's department, ILR, is housed, and I'm a little surprised by this self-confidence that I've not encountered before. "Smooth Operator" shows himself to be possessed of an authority that is new to me. He talks easily about the Princeton win. Yes, they expected Princeton to make a run at some point. They knew that they were going to have to counter that. Yes, this season's Cornell team has a good feel about it.

Keller, Manon, and Nas are all ILR majors. Teaching in Ives, I feel like I'm intruding on their institutional turf. I'll have to tread carefully on Tuesdays and Thursdays.

With regret, and only because I have to teach, I say goodbye to Mr. Boothby, as I am wont to address him.

January 27, 2024.

The only player on the Cornell team, to my mind, who even comes close to Boothby as a pure shooter is his fellow senior, the Brigham City, Utah, native Max Watson. Cooper Noard, however, might have a thing or two to say about that. And I won't even dare to solicit Nas's view of my judgment. There's a reason Nas wears the #1 jersey.

Jay Fiegen, Jacob Beccles, Adam Tsang Hinton, DJ Nix, and Guy Ragland Jr. all make key contributions at some point in the Princeton game.

Brian Earl's Team.

I like this Cornell team. *Really like these guys—from the coaching staff to the guys who ride the pine.*

In our household, Zeke, Manon, and Nas are held in the highest esteem. Zeke, given his relationship with Ezra, occupies pride of place, but Manon and Nas are not far behind. Nas and Zeke, as well as Nas and Beccles, as already mentioned, have come to a few of Ezra's games.

"Go to work, E!" Nas yells from the stands, completely uninhibited, that borderline illegal laugh smeared all over his face. "Let's go, E!" Nas only speaks in sentences that end in an exclamation mark or, as is more likely, several exclamation marks.

And Chris, with his charisma—well, everybody loves Chris, right?

However, the player I identify with most is Sean Hansen. I've nicknamed Sean "The Bricklayer."

When I tell Zeke this, in typical Zeke fashion, he seizes the moment to impugn Hansen's shot-making abilities. "Bricklayer?" Zeke queries. "Is that because he lays bricks?"—a pejorative for a bad shot or simply an ugly shot that comes up empty.

Anthony Mason was given the nickname "Brick" by the Knicks color commentator Walt Clyde Frazier specifically because of that propensity. Mason, however, would go on to improve his shot. It would never become a thing of beauty. It did, however, lose its (more) unsightly aspects. Plus, Brick was so strong that he did most of his damage under the basket, anyway, both as a scorer and, obviously, as a rebounder, so that the aesthetics of his shot were easy to overlook.

Sean Hansen is a lunch-pail, hard-hat, put-in-an-honest-shift-every-time-he's-on-the-court kind of player.

Lunch-pail player. Like the hardworking players on those much-vaunted defenses on those 1987 and 1991 New York Giants Super Bowl winning teams. Guys like Pepper Johnson, Leonard Marshall, Carl Banks, Everson Walls, coached by Bill Parcells. New Jersey native Parcells. Banks and company were good players but not exactly stars who brought everything to every play on defense. They came to work, every day.

On those Giants defenses, Lawrence Taylor was the star. "LT," as he is popularly known, was a team player and formed a formidable linebacker corps with his colleagues. But LT, with that preternatural anticipation, his strength and ingenuity, well, LT always just seemed to do his own thing. To great effect. #56. LT was special. Greatest defensive player I have ever seen.

An engineering major, Hansen is that Cornell student who is interested in the world. On New Year's Eve in 2023, we have Zeke, Chris, and Hansen over for dinner. Sean is the only one who asks about the books and artwork in our house.

Zeke and Chris are goofing off with Ezra—that is, when they're not checking their phones.

4:45 p.m., January 27, 2024.

Zeke, donning a white T-shirt and gray sweats, beanie balanced nonchalantly on his head, comes strutting out of the locker room.

After the pain of last season's home loss to Princeton, this is a big day for the undefeated Cornell Big Red basketball team.

Zeke tells Ezra and me that Hansen, that pillar of sanity and senior responsibility, cautioned the team in the locker room. "It's only one game," Sean said. But Zeke's too hyped, and he just laughed off Hansen's caution. Like a good coach, our Mr. Hansen reminds the team to take one game at a time. Don't get too high after a victory; don't sink too low after a defeat.

Hansen is trying to make sure that the team gets ready to play Dartmouth and Harvard on the upcoming road trip to New Hampshire and Massachusetts—Dartmouth on February 2, with Harvard on tap the following night.

Of course, Zeke knows this, but for now, he just wants to revel in this triumph.

I'm happy for Zeke, Manon, Hansen, Nas, and the team. They deserve it. This afternoon, they outplayed Princeton, and then some.

But, as important as this victory is for Brian Earl's team, I'm still reeling. There are some losses that can never be overcome.

A Saturday in September 1990.

I've been in the United States for a little over a year.

It's around 2:00 P.M., and I'm passing by Micawber's Bookstore on Nassau Street,[18] the main drag in Princeton. I'm new in town, having just moved from Columbia University's Morningside Heights neighborhood, so I'm trying to get a feel for the place.

Nassau Street is, as far as I can tell, unusually quiet. But, since I only arrived at the end of August, I pay the lack of foot traffic no mind.

I'm looking at the books displayed in Micawber's windows when a professor from my department happens past.

The professor knows that I am a sport's fan from a brief conversation we'd had a few months or so ago.

He is therefore surprised to see me outside Micawber's.

"You're not at the game?" he asks.

"The game?" I reply, completely unsure as to what game it is that this professor thinks I should be watching.

"The football game," he enlightens me. "Princeton's playing."

I tell him that I had no idea that there was a game going on.

And then, in a moment, my utter ignorance about the intense relationship between the institution of higher learning—Princeton, in this case—and those who attend it is revealed to me.

I'm about to be given a quick primer on "rah-rah" culture, Princeton style.

"This," the professor says to me, "is a very rah-rah town."

I am sure that I look utterly confused. I look utterly confused because I am utterly confused.

What in the good Lord's name is "rah-rah?" Am I even spelling it correctly in my head?

My confusion is obvious, so the professor proceeds to explain: "It means that everyone here goes to support the team when they play."

OK, but how does that amount to "rah-rah"?

Since I am clearly still confused, he goes on: "They're all invested in Princeton. They wear school colors. It's an opportunity for them to demonstrate their school spirit."

Fair enough. *Rah-rah* is what binds the individual, for life, to the school, to its colors. It's what makes alumni wistful. It's what makes alumni commit to having their children follow in their institutional footsteps (they don't call them "legacies" for nothing). It's what makes them sing, loudly and boisterously, the school song. It brings out their inner intra-Ivy animus and sometimes—more often than they might care to admit—their not-so-inner Ivy animus.

Rah-rah is not only about loyalty. It is, I suspect, about the superiority of your school, cloaked in the mantle of athletic competition. Or, maybe, not cloaked at all.

At Cornell men's hockey games, distinguished Cornell faculty yell at the opposing goaltender, all of nineteen years old, "You suck! You suck!"

LFC fans are renowned for their biting Scouser wit. And they rarely spare opposing players the sharp end of their wit. But those opposing players are, for the most part, grown men—professionals, earning a living.

Beneath the pretense of civility lies, close to the surface, a deep-seated belief in how your institution, in terms of education and influence (its range of networks, in Washington, DC; on Wall Street; from sea to shining sea), bests all others.

Rah-rah is celebrating your own importance, affirming it, in public, for the world to see—for the small world, the ice rink, the basketball arena, the football stadium, to see and hear.

Go Tigers!

One can only imagine how much rah-rah and school spirit it takes if you have even the slightest twinge of uncertainty about the status of your institution.

That may be why, after long dominating college athletics, Ivy League schools, liberal arts colleges, contented themselves with their influence, with their unsurpassed networks. Those networks, out of which is constructed an unrivaled access to power, privilege, and wealth, make the athletic prowess of the big state schools a matter of no consequence.

The University of Alabama may have won yet another national championship in college football, but how many Supreme Court Justices can they boast? Justices Samuel Alito, Elena Kagan, and Sonia Sotomayor are all Princeton alums.

Roll over, Tide, Roll over.

But at the core of that loyalty is an abiding affinity with the institution. A bond that is, if not unbreakable (although it is for many an alum, I'm sure), strong enough to endure. At the core of that loyalty is what English public-school types call the "old school tie." A sense of shared values, civic virtues. A way of looking at the world that is held in common and held in trust, sometimes in sacred trust—not simply friendships, important or instrumental as those might be, but a deeper commitment to being in the world in a certain way.

A form of tribalism all its own.

As a Liverpool fan, I thought I knew a thing or two about tribalism. I hate Manchester United, Arsenal, Chelsea, Everton. But all of that at a distance. Like my long-distance love.

A form of tribalism that works in such a way that it both centers the individual and decenters the individual by locating the individual in a series of networks that might exceed the narrow self-interest that is the "old boys network."

Ties that transcend all kinds of barriers. Ties that allow individuals to overcome all manner of individual differences.

The sense that there is something that is greater than the self.

Something worth cheering for; something that adds to the pathos of rah-rah a deeper dimension, perhaps even a dimension to which no rah-rah chant can admit.

A mode of being in relation to other human beings that speaks—or sings—of human need. The need to be in community with, the need to at once acknowledge the self's insignificance in the cosmos and to overcome that insignificance through maintaining a bond with those with whom one has shared a coming-of-age experience.

Go Tigers, without the exclamation mark. A modulated exhortation that insists on being spoken quietly, thoughtfully. That exhortation that can inflect "rah-rah" with meaning.

Of this form of institutional tribalism, I know nothing. A babe in arms, I am.

Brian Earl Is a Princeton Man. I Am Not a Princeton Man. Maybe Brian Earl Is Not a Princeton Man.

Brian Earl is a Princeton man.

Other alumni include: F. Scott Fitzgerald, Teddy Roosevelt, John F. Kennedy, Michelle Obama, Syngman Rhee, and Brooke Shields. So are Lee Iacocca, Eugene O'Neill, Donald Rumsfeld, James Madison, and John Rawls.

One of my teachers in graduate school, Cornel West, received his PhD from Princeton. Before that, he graduated from Harvard *summa cum laude*. In 1994, West left Princeton to return to Cambridge, Massachusetts, to teach at his alma mater.

It was, as many know, a rocky tenure, clashing as Cornel did with the then–Harvard president Larry Summers, but Cornel's capacious, charismatic mind surely did much to enliven staid Harvard. He made his Princeton classrooms an engaging, effervescent place to be. The graduate seminar I took with him in the spring of 1992 on the black radical tradition attracted students from all over. Some took the train from Philadelphia to Princeton, while others found their way south from pastures further afield, such as New Haven, Connecticut, home to Yale.

But West, one of contemporary America's most publicly recognizable intellectuals and, in the fall of 2023, a presidential candidate, is *not* a Princeton man. I am not a Princeton man. Having a Princeton degree is, of course, only the entry line qualification for being a Princeton man.

However, my experience at Princeton brought home to me the truth of Princeton's institutional hierarchy. As we know, Princeton has no professional schools—an institutional decision that carries significant weight.

What this means is that the institution is committed to undergraduate education. This has fostered an institutional culture in which undergraduates, at least during the years I spent there, know their institutional centrality. The university revolves around them.

It revolves around their education, around their eating clubs.

If you don't believe me, just take a gander at Princeton alum F. Scott Fitzgerald's *The Great Gatsby*. Although *The Great Gatsby* is set at Yale, Fitzgerald drew heavily on his Princeton years to depict upper-class life at the top end of the Ivy League ladder. Fitzgerald's novel brings home to its readers the immense sense of entitlement and privilege that pervades the ethos at an institution such as Princeton. It also reveals the petty, fractious, and destructive underside of Ivy culture at schools such as Princeton and Yale.

Princeton's eating clubs are notorious. They are where the rich kids take their meals, mingle with their own. Princeton, in case you didn't know, has no Greek system—no fraternities, no sororities. They have eating clubs, a form of undergraduate social organization that is as far removed from the cliqueish, pay-for-your-friends world of frats and sororities as you could imagine.

If only.

Williams banned the Greek system in the late 1970s.

For Princeton's eating clubs, substitute team sports at Williams.

Speaking of the Greek system—if you're at an elite institution and your ostensible reason for joining a frat or a sorority is for "networking," isn't that already a sign of failure? What's the value of your degree? How much more of a leg up does an Ivy League graduate really need?

In my experience, Princeton only lets its hair down once a year. And what a spectacle it is when this happens. It goes by the name of "Reunion."

And, boy, is it an anthropological marvel. Everyone, or just about every Princeton alum still ambulatory, seems to be in attendance.

Every graduating class gets all dolled up in their distinctive version of black and orange—striped blazers, striped trousers, boaters, straw hats, floppy caps, one more charmingly gaudy than the next. Yes, there are some aesthetic eyesores, but it remains, nonetheless, a remarkable spectacle.

Just watch the ruling class, the class of 19—edition, strut their stuff and march, in various stages of inebriation, in their regalia before adoring crowds.

At either the back or the rear of some classes, a spiffy car, one that rolled off the assembly line in the year in which that class graduated, will invariably make an appearance.

There are some nice wheels, I must admit. Some of the vintage types are in mint condition. I cast envious glances in that direction, especially toward those that parade slowly with the top down.

"I'd like to get me one of those."

There's something different about the class of 1970, though: women. Princeton first admitted women in 1969. Eight female transfers would graduate in 1970.[19]

I observed this spectacle a couple of times while I was in graduate school and always felt a certain awe and an undeniable alienation. Princeton is where I went to school, but this was not my world. I would never belong here, not like *them*—*they* all seemed so at home. This was *their* place. I was given the privilege of observing them, safe in my anonymity.

I never had the sense that *they* saw me observing *them*.

But maybe they were just too hammered.

After all, as an undergraduate working one of the events remarked to me, with some incredulity, "More beer is consumed at a Princeton Reunion than at the Indy 500."

Take that, you Dale Earnhardt fans. Indy crowds could take a lesson in consumption from the swaying bands of orange-and-black marchers.

It may be, then, that an institution where you don't register sociopolitically, at least not with any significance, is the perfect place to be a graduate student. That's how it seems to me now, at least.

In fact, rather than feeling slighted at being denied the status of Princeton man, I found it to be quite the best thing about being a Princeton graduate student.

Because the institution did not revolve around graduate students, we, the children of a lesser Princeton god, were left to our devices.

We did only, at least in my day, one semester of teaching, so our interactions with the undergraduates were limited. Some upperclassmen took seminars with grad students. They seemed a nice-enough bunch—bright, well-read, worldly; in short, they were mainly the moneyed ruling class. They were restrained and not flashy with their wealth and well-mannered to a fault. Their world was alien to me but not in the least unpleasant. We lived in our world, while they ruled institutional life, always in the most unarguable but understated fashion.

It was their institution.

An insanely well-resourced institution, Princeton provided a decent stipend, good health care, and support for summer research.

I loved my time there for one reason above all others: the institution left us alone to do our work.

Not only was our status that of second-class citizens, but because we lived in off-campus housing, either in repurposed Quonset huts (Butler) or nondescript high rises (Lawrence Apartments), we did not register socially.

Occasionally, we made a weekend pilgrimage to New York City, at once aghast at this little enclave of privilege in which we were living yet marveling at this curious institutional animal to which we were entrusting our present and, of course, our professional futures.

I could inhabit this place without it occupying too much of my time. I felt a strange affinity to it.

Or a not-so-strange affinity. They left us alone, free to make our nondescript way in their world. We would leave no noticeable imprint on their lives. They, on the other hand, would leave us forever marked by our time at Princeton.

Was their ability to pass so easily over us, mere graduate students, a source of solace? Did they pity us? I have not yet been able to decide. Mostly, I imagine, they were indifferent.

But I could have asked for no more. They left us alone. I formed intellectual habits at Princeton—reading, writing, and thinking habits that I retain to this day and might never have formed anywhere else. Who knows? I found myself there and I took, insofar as it is possible to avail myself fully of what is on offer, what I needed. And, perhaps, I even took that which I did not know I needed. Princeton may have given me things for which I will never be able to account, as it surely took from me things I cannot know and might never know.

The ledger that is the accounting of my time in graduate school will remain as it is—open, with debits and credits on either side. The ledger will remain unbalanced, as it should.

I know only this: I have not returned to Princeton, New Jersey, since I defended my dissertation.

I have no plans to, either.

Returning is work best left for Princeton men and women.

Theirs is the real and enduring institutional bond. I can't imagine putting together a garish outfit in orange and black.

I'm perfectly fine with my Princeton-adjacent status.

But to my Cornell students, I dissemble—sort of.

I don't claim to be a Princeton man. I just say that I went to Princeton, a "real Ivy."

Perhaps it is the realest of them all.

Brian Earl is sheepish when I make the distinction between us.

To his credit, there is nothing of the Princeton man about him.

But he did play on a historic Princeton team.

Something dawns on me while talking with Brian: not all Princeton men *are* actually Princeton men, or want to be Princeton men, or understand themselves as such.

Sometimes, it's just where they went to college, which is, of course, never a matter of "just," but still . . .

Sometimes, it's just where they went to college and played on a #13 seed team that beat a #4 seed team.

There is, undoubtedly, something *trés* cool about that.

I wonder if Brian's teammates, especially Mitch Henderson, the current Tiger's men's head coach, and Sydney Johnson think of themselves as Princeton men.

The über-Princeton basketball man Bill Bradley might, I imagine, understand himself to be a Princeton man.

Bill Bradley is a Princeton Renaissance man: star athlete, Rhodes Scholar, member of the 1973 New York Knicks championship team, New Jersey senator, U.S. presidential candidate.

In a different, quieter, more intense register, Brian Earl puts me in mind of Bradley. Brian has about him a sense of intellectual acuity, personal modesty, and athletic honesty, an openness to the world that Bradley must have had and must still have—the Rhodes Scholar who formed a critical part of that second Knicks championship team with the likes of Georgia native Walt Clyde Frazier, the greatest Knick of all, and the *ur*-hippie, the Christian fundamentalist's son from North Dakota who would leave his mark on the NBA as the Zen meister par excellence, Phil Jackson.

There are Princeton men to whom one warms.

With whom the difference between being and not being a Princeton man seems not to matter quite so much.

Or even to matter at all.

Sometimes, it's just the first moment of connection in a longer conversation.

Sometimes, if you're lucky, you find out that there are many other things you'd rather talk about—as long as it's about basketball.

4:45 P.M., January 27, 2024.

With every passing hour, this loss is seeping into and settling in my bones. And a loss of the magnitude I'm enduring has no place in this pumped-up gym at Cornell—the giddy after-party.

It may, however, be the only place where loss and the celebration of victory find cohabitation.

1:36 p.m., January 26, 2024.

After all, news of that loss began the previous afternoon with a text from Brian Earl.

His text reads: "He needs a vacation." He included a link to an article titled "Jurgen Klopp Is Leaving Liverpool This Summer. Now What?"

The *he* in question, as you already know, is Jürgen Norbert Klopp, manager of LFC.

Come the end of February 2024, I will have supported this club—my club—for fifty-four years. Klopp became manager, as I've mentioned, in October 2015.

He revived a Liverpool club adrift.

The fans—all of us, from the city of Liverpool to those who inhabit, as I do, far-flung little college towns in upstate New York—warmed to him. We fell in love with him.

And now he is leaving.

As things will turn out, there was a subtext to Brian Earl's text.

Klopp would be taking with him that infectious energy, that bond with the Kop (the Liverpool fans who occupy the historic Kop End of Liverpool's home ground, Anfield). No longer would he be seen walking over to the Kop at the end of the game, pumping his fist in their direction three times before placing his right hand on the LFC crest, the Liver bird. Klopp knows holiness.

I'm close to tears, unable to speak.

The best are full of passionate intensity?

Lead Story on the Six O'clock News in England: January 26, 2024.

"Jürgen Klopp Resigns."

The news tonight, from Liverpool to London, is that the killing of Palestinians in Gaza will not be the headline tonight.

Instead, the headline is that Klopp has announced that, come the end of the season, he will step down from his role after almost nine years.

Klopp is telling us now, so that we can prepare ourselves for it. As if that's supposed to make us feel better.

As if such a heads-up can make us feel less numb.

I get on my e-bike and ride aimlessly.

#20S.

It's a cold, biting Friday in Ithaca. There's no snow, but it's a cold that cuts to your bones.
    I am going to feel that bitter cold on the bike.
    No matter. Before I get on the bike, I change my shirt and jacket. I'd walked our dog earlier and had dressed for it. But the news of Klopp's imminent departure makes the weather a secondary concern.
    I put on a Liverpool jersey from the 2017–18 season. It's the technically gifted midfielder Adam Lallana's shirt, #20.
    Lallana played for LFC from July 2014 to June 2020. He won everything, including the Premier League title and the Champion's League.
    If there is any LFC player who, for me, epitomized what Jürgen Klopp expected of his team, it is Lallana. Slightly built, Lallana was wonderfully adept with the ball at his feet; he was able to command small spaces and create with just a single flick or an imaginative touch. He picked up more than his share of injuries while he was with us, but I loved watching Lallana go to work. Unselfish, he'd drop back deep into the midfield, pick up the ball, and do the simple things—the short pass, the smart one-twos (when the same two players interchange passes between themselves), the quick layoff.
    Over my #20 shirt, I put on a retro zip-up LFC top, an Adidas top that dates to the 1980s.
    I should be freezing as I ride my bike, but I'm so disconnected from the material world that I'm hardly aware of the temperature—it's probably in the mid-thirties.

There might be something poetic about Klopp's leaving being announced today and my donning a #20 LFC shirt. Especially today.

Nip wears #20 in honor of his maternal grandfather, Ron Juffer, who wore the number in his playing days as a high schooler in northwestern Iowa, Sioux Center, and as a college standout at Morningside College in nearby Sioux City, Iowa. "Little Ronnie Juffer," they used to call him, a star local athlete who excelled at basketball, baseball, and tennis and a revered coach in all three sports at Northwestern College, where he taught for almost fifty years.

Such a legend is Ron Juffer. In his late seventies and early eighties, my late father-in-law played pickup basketball with the grandkids of students he'd taught. He played H-O-R-S-E with middle schoolers in the Northwestern gym into his early eighties. He hustled those kids, we used to joke, *The Color of Money* playing out in Northwestern's Student Center (the RSC, or the Rowenhorst Student Center), without the money. Players on the Northwestern basketball team, high schoolers, middle schoolers, and anyone else who happened to be in the gym could get roped into playing with Ron Juffer and then go home to tell their parents, who had probably had the same experience.

The RSC was where Ron Juffer shot hoops, played one-on-one, shot pool, and played table tennis with all of his grandchildren and Jane, his younger daughter, who inherited her father's undying faith in the left-hand hook shot. "Indefensible," they both agreed.

Once he reached that venerable age where he could no longer defend against the drive, the Juffer Rules kicked in: no driving on Ron, or "Pops," lifelong Chicago Cubs fans, as his grandkids called him. Like their grandfather, all except for Ezra (he got my hapless, miserable New York Mets instead) are Cubbies loyalists.

Appropriately, Northwestern named an athletic facility in honor of him and his wife, Peg: The Ron and Peg Juffer Fieldhouse.

Stalwart Northwestern fans, and a Peg a librarian whose name now adorns an athletic facility.

Adam Lallana, Ezra Farred, Rodney Dean Juffer: A trinity of #20s brought together by Jürgen Klopp.

And then there was a quartet, completed by Sean Hansen, Cornell men's basketball #20.

If I could snag only one Cornell jersey, it'd be the Bricklayer's.

January 27, 2024.

Cornell beats Princeton.
    The Knicks beat the Miami Heat.
    Julius Randle dislocates his right shoulder. Randle will be out for at least three weeks.
    Ezra says he'll go back to watching the Knicks.
    There is little good about the state of Florida, and much of what is so distasteful about the state can be found in the Miami Heat.
    No seasons. Repugnant conservatism. In what other state would the governor pick a fight with Disney? Who puts their dukes up against Mickey Mouse? Bugs and swamps, alligators and swamps. Little concern for environmental degradation.
    Too much time for tanning.
    Here's looking at you, Pat Riley. (Riley is a former Knicks coach, as we know. But what I haven't told you is that he is the kind of basketball guy who resigns via fax—a class act, that Pat. Steve Summers, WFAN's sportscaster, indicted Riley's escape from New York with a reptilian metaphor: "He left town like a slithering snake.")
    The Heat's Jimmy Butler[20] has proven himself to be a Knick killer.
    Butler's *that* kind of player: arrogant and unlikeable, unless he is on your team, like Marcus Smart when he was on the Boston Celtics or the Golden State Warriors' Draymond Green. To his credit, Butler is (only) smarmy arrogant; Green's borderline dirty, and sometimes he crosses the threshold.

It is now possible to feel sorry for Marcus Smart, who was traded from the Celtics to the basketball cesspit that is the Memphis Grizzlies. It couldn't have happened to a nicer guy.

As a fan, *you* want *your* team to beat Jimmy Butler.

Up in the Heat executive suite is Alonzo Mourning, the only Georgetown University alum (who played for the legendary John Thompson) who curls your toes.

I loved John Thompson. I loved watching him coach and rooted for the Georgetown Hoyas when he was in charge. John Thompson was the first African American coach to win the NCAA title. Thompson was academically demanding of his players. Of all Thompson's Hall of Fame players (the likes of Ewing, Dikembe Mutombo, Alonzo Mourning), Allen Iverson is the only one not to graduate.

Ewing, Mutombo, Iverson—no matter who those Georgetown boys played for professionally (Mutombo, the Denver Nuggets and the Atlanta Hawks; Iverson, the Philadelphia 76ers), you bore them no ill will.

This is not so with Zo.

Every time I look at Mourning, dark thoughts cross my mind.

There is an unpleasant smugness about Zo. He does not strike me as the kind of guy you want to hang around.

I conclude that Zo's too brooding and Riley's too slick. This is more than sufficient reason to dislike the Heat.

The Knicks beat the Heat—no small feat—but today, that is not enough.

The Game after *The* Announcement.

Tomorrow, Sunday, January 28, Liverpool plays their first game since Klopp's announcement.

They are playing Norwich City, a team in the division below Liverpool, known as the Championship (when I was growing up it was just the Second Division—I much preferred that designation), at Anfield. It's a fourth round in the FA Cup.

All Liverpool fans will be up for that—and down because of it. It is Match Day 1 of the beginning of the end of the Klopp era.

LFC: Three Names.

Bill Shankly (The Shankly Gates), Bob Paisley (The Paisley Gates), Kenny Dalglish (The Sir Kenny Dalglish Stand)—these are the three greatest managers in the club's history.

And then there were four.

How will we honor Jürgen, our German Scouser? (Scouser is the name given to Liverpool natives.)

From Cape Town, South Africa, I came to know—via print media—the legend of the Scot Shankly, a manager given to memorable quotes and hubris.

After LFC wins the FA Cup in 1965 for the first time in their history, the team and the coaching staff treat the fans to an open bus parade through the city. Shankly looks on joyously at the sea of red that lines the city's streets.

Observing this spectacle, Shankly, never at a loss for words, turns to one of the players and asks, with urgency in his voice, "That Chinaman, that Chinaman, what's his name?" "You mean Chairman Mao," the bemused player replies.[21]

"Chairman Mao," intones Shankly, the Scottish socialist, to the thousands of adoring Liverpool faithful. "Chairman Mao never saw such a sea of red." The crowd goes wild.

Bob Paisley, a manager not given to anything like verbal excess, is my favorite LFC manager. A son of England's cold and blustery North-East, Hetton-le-Hole, Paisley was a scholar of the game. He took notes, carefully. He scrutinized defeats perhaps more carefully than victories. He used his notes to his advantage and was a master of strategy, the manager who made Liverpool a footballing force not only in England but all over Europe.

Kenny Dalglish, a Scot, was, for many LFC fans, the club's greatest player and was a superb manager.

He was a man and a manager undone, as I've related, by the tragedy that was Hillsborough—a man and a manager who bore the weight of a city's tragedy.

Kenny and his wife, Marina, went to funeral after funeral in the wake of Hillsborough.

He still smiles puckishly, does our Kenny, but who can know what the effect of ninety-six people dying, ninety-six of your fans, Scousers who lived, and then died, for Liverpool, does to a man?

Especially a man such as Kenny, for whom LFC meant everything—maybe even more than his first club, Glasgow Celtic of Scotland?

Jürgen Klopp is the perfect blend of his three predecessors. Klopp possesses something like Shankly's verbal dexterity, which was always laced with a mischievousness. Klopp is intelligent and thoughtful, like Paisley—Bob Paisley, the supreme note taker. Like Dalglish, Klopp is endowed with the common touch.

He understands the Scousers. He loves them. They reciprocate beyond measure.

Klopp's leaving. Liverpool fans the world over, but starting in the city itself, break down and cry when they hear the news. The LFC staff—not the coaches, but the folks who maintain Anfield—cannot help themselves. Klopp admits that the tears flowed when he made his announcement to them.

During the game against Norwich, the fans serenade Klopp, his name ringing from the rafters. He has expressly pleaded with the fans not to do so.

It is a battle he is not likely to win.

Klopp, the LFC three-in-one: Shankly, Paisley, Dalglish. The Holy Trinity. And then there were four.

January 28, 2024.

There's an FA Cup tie at Anfield (full name: Anfield Road), Liverpool's home ground. This is the first game in the beginning of the end; Liverpool beats Norwich City, 5–2.

It's not even close.

LFC are through to the fifth round of the FA Cup.

ESPN's Mark Ogden remarks on the "strange atmosphere" at Anfield.

The commentator Ian Darke, who has a sobriety about him, a dry but by no means dull way of describing the game as it unfolds, sounds more austere than ever today. It's been a "traumatic week," he intones quietly; it's the "end of a traumatic week."

What exactly do you mean by "week," Mr. Darke?

It's been forty-eight hours.

Traumatized though I am, it's Mark Ogden who catches my mood.

This is indeed "strange" for me. After almost two years away, I watch but cannot quite give myself over to LFC, much as I would like to—for a second time.

I'm not indifferent to Klopp leaving. I'm not indifferent to the pain that washes over Anfield. I am deeply moved. I feel it. I share it.

And yet it remains, just ever so slightly, beyond me.

I am fully aware of this pain, this brutal reality that Klopp is leaving, but I can't go all the way back.

I want Liverpool to win.

It's that indefinable remove I cannot, can no longer, overcome.

January 30, 2024.

The New York Knicks beat the Utah Jazz, 118–113, for their eighth straight win.
    They end the month of January with an NBA-leading record of 14–2, tying the franchise record for second best in a single month.
    What was the last Knicks team to boast such a record?
    No need to guess. Yes, it was the 1994 edition of the Knicks. And yes, it was in January, exactly thirty years ago.
    Ewing, Oakley, Mason—their team went to the NBA finals.[22]
    I'm not holding my breath.
    The best lack all conviction.
    For what it's worth, with Randle out, Ezra's happier.
    Apparently, Randle could be out for a while.
    As of February 10, the date of Randle's return remains uncertain.
    January 27 presents a trifecta for Ezra: Cornell men win, Knicks win, and Randle's on the injured list.
    Tomorrow, January 28, I'll watch my first Liverpool game in twenty months.

Pep Guardiola on Sleeping Easy.

Manchester City manager Josep "Pep" Guardiola responds to the news by declaring that with Klopp's resignation from Liverpool, he will now be able to sleep easier on the night before Manchester City and Liverpool do battle.

This will be a new experience for Guardiola. Heretofore it had been, in Pep's words, "a nightmare."

All LFC fans know Pep's sentiment is by no means particular to him. All of the English Premier League and all of Europe's elite football clubs are no doubt in agreement.

Klopp, Pep goes on to say, had been his "best rival."

Pep, and Pep alone, can say this.

Pep, who was massively successful as a manager at his native FC Barcelona in Spain (2008–12) and then had an equally impressive stint at Bayern München in Germany, is currently cock-a-hoop in the English Premier League. He has waged many a battle against Klopp.

While Pep was in charge of Bayern (2013–15), Klopp was manager at Borussia Dortmund (2008–15).

In October 2015, Klopp was appointed to the Liverpool job. Nine months later, in July 2016, Guardiola became Manchester City manager.

They had managerial careers in which each was the other's main antagonist.

The tightly wound Guardiola and the free-spirited Klopp were close comrades, men who genuinely like each other, coaches committed to playing open, attractive football.

They have their foibles, Klopp and Pep, but there is none of Rafa's prickliness, none of Alex Ferguson's (former Manchester United manager) boorishness, none of Arsène Wenger's (former Arsenal manager) faux intellectuality and haughtiness.

It is a thing of sadness that they will do battle no more. There will be no more pitting wits, each probing for weakness in the other, each trying to get under the other's skin.

Each admiring the other.

Pep Knows.

Four seasons (2008–12): that is how long Pep Guardiola managed his beloved FC Barcelona, for whom he had starred as a player from 1990 to 2001.

Those four years, according to Pep, felt like an eternity.

On a rolling contract that could be renewed at the end of every season, he stepped down after four seasons—four very successful seasons. Pep won La Liga titles. He won the Champions League. He brought home to Catalunya the Copa Del Rey (the King's Cup, the Spanish equivalent of the FA Cup). At the end of those four long seasons, he was, Pep said, "tired."

That is exactly what Klopp said. And his tenure at Liverpool will, at its conclusion, have been more than twice as long as Pep's at his native Barcelona.

Pep Guardiola not only played for and managed Barcelona (that wonderful team that Pep molded, which included Lionel Messi, Gerard Pique, and Sergio Busquets), but he is deeply invested in the Catalan nationalist project and is an outspoken advocate for it.

Even though he represented Spain on forty-seven occasions (1992–2001), he also played seven games for the Catalonia team (1995–2005).

In the long aftermath of the Spanish Civil War (1936–39) and the defeat of the Spanish Republic by the reactionary forces of General Francisco Franco, the Catalan nationalist cause—along with that of Basques—has always drawn partisans of a leftist persuasion. After Liverpool, Barcelona is my second team,[23] in no small measure because the history of FC Barcelona, which is so enmeshed in the Republican cause, pits it so strongly against the historic Francoism of Real Madrid. Rendered reductively, and far too simplistically, for me, Barça will always be the anti-fascist team.

However, it is precisely because there is so much invested by the Catalans in Barça that the team has to bear the burden of overrepresentation, a concept I have developed more fully elsewhere.[24] Every Barça triumph in La Liga, every victory over the hated Real, is overwrought by forces far beyond the confines of the football pitch.

This is why those of a leftist political persuasion support the team, no matter its missteps, although one's misgivings tend to add up.

But Barça is not Real Madrid.

Sometimes that can tide you over.

What a burden that must be for a (football) man as historically aware, as politically astute, as ideologically wired as Josep Guardiola Sala (his full name)—to know how much depends upon each Barça game.

Over four years as manager, to say nothing of his eleven years as player, to which we must add his year's tenure (2007–8) as manager of Barça's B team, must have collectively worn Pep down. Tired him right out. Taken its toll on him.

To manage Barça is to be the figurehead of an ethnonationalist struggle.

Barça *is* the Catalan struggle against Castilian hegemony. Every defeat, especially to Real Madrid, wounds an entire people's psyche.

In his role as manager, Pep was the spearhead of that ethnonationalist movement; as a graduate of its famed La Masia (Barça's youth academy) and former player, he was instructed into its meaning. But, as a native Catalan, any such instruction would have been, in large measure, superfluous.

It's no wonder he took a year's sabbatical after giving up the managerial reigns at Barça, decamping to New York.

In 2013, Pep returned to management, and once more he found himself in an ideological cauldron, this time taking up an appointment with the German giants, FC Bayern Munich. Munich, of course, is the capital of Bavaria, and to be Bavarian is to embody its own brand of regional particularism—nay, regional superiority. Bayern Munich is the most successful club in the history of German football. They are widely reviled by all other teams for both their superiority and their success. Bayern also, together with Real Madrid, AC Milan (Italy), and Liverpool, ranks among the Continental elite as one of the most successful clubs in Europe.

Despite all the expectations that attach to being the club's manager, Bayern must have come as a relief to Pep. Yes, the expectation that he would win the Bundesliga every year, season after season, must have represented its own burden, especially with as formidable a foe as Klopp (as manager of Borussia Dortmund) would have been when Dortmund did battle against Bayern and especially with the expectation that Bayern would challenge, every year, season after season, for the Champions League trophy. That was no small ask, but it was probably easily more bearable to someone as naturally driven and competitive as Pep.

After Barça and Bayern, however, managing Manchester City, a team not inscribed with the same ethnonationalist or regional identity as those of his previous appointment, has surely come as a relief.

All the expectations borne by Pep in Manchester are of his own creation. And he has thrived at the Etihad Stadium in Manchester, putting City's hated rivals Manchester United to the sword, increasingly with consummate ease. Pep has delivered trophy-laden season after trophy-laden season. Manchester City is not only the best team in the English Premier League, with only Liverpool as a genuine and sustained rival, but they are—on current form—arguably the best team in all of Europe and, indeed, world club football.[25]

It may be easier for Pep to excel at Man City because he is not of the Mancs, as the club's fans are called. It may be easier for Pep to endure in his job at the Etihad because he is able to operate, for the first time in his career (both as player and manager), at a psychological remove.

He is in charge at the Etihad, but he is not *of* the Mancs.

Catalonia is in Pep's bones. Nay, he is a Catalan to his marrow.

Such intense identification will, sooner or later, take its toll.

Managing Man City is, of course, by no means a stress-free job. But the toll it takes is professional, not personal. And therein lies all the difference. The professional will grind a manager down, wear him out physically and emotionally, but it will not touch his soul.

Jürgen Klopp Knows What Pep Knows. Twice Over.

When Klopp announced in the spring of 2015 that he would be stepping down as manager of Borussia Dortmund, I had no doubt that his next appointment would be LFC.

If you've ever visited the city of Dortmund, you would understand why I could so confidently make that prediction. The similarities between the cities, Liverpool and Dortmund, are striking.

They are both working-class cities devastated by post-industrialism. Dortmund was badly bombed during World War II because it was the hub of German military manufacturing. Dortmund has about it a rough feel; it is a city that has known hard times, a city with a long memory of economic decline.

So too is Liverpool—in fact, even more so. Liverpool, a working-class city in England's northwest, is a city that bore, like other parts of the English north, the brunt of the Thatcherite attack on trade unions (the Liverpool dock workers strike of 1984 proved immensely costly to the labor movement in Britain), the laying waste of the Welfare State.

But Liverpool, even more than a city such as Manchester, has a strong sense of itself and a very long history of being vehemently opposed to the notion of "England." For Scousers, "England" stands as the bastion of southern conservatism (that is, "England" as a national entity that turns on London and its environs; that is, "England" as an antiradical formation hostile to the Northern working classes).

LFC players, it is said (and widely believed to be true), care less about the English national team than they do about the fortunes of LFC. The city of Liverpool is in England, geographically, but not *of* it. When Trent Alexander-Arnold represents England, he is entirely silent during the playing of the English national anthem. His lips do not move. In that moment, one knows that Trent is a true Scouser. As if we ever doubted that.

Scousers are understood to be a geopolitical entity unto themselves.

Coming from Dortmund, Klopp grasped the city's and LFC's outsiderness, its self-imposed alienation from Englishness, intuitively.

What is more, Klopp embraced it. He threw himself into the spirit of a city that conceives of itself as not only economically neglected and politically distinct but as embodying a very different spirit—the spirit of radical opposition to southern hegemony. To play for LFC is to know what it means to stick it to the folks from London, with their Tory (Conservative Party, England's equivalent of the Republican Party in this country) sensibility, their disdain for the people of Liverpool, their contempt for the impoverished city and its long-suffering population.

If, as we said, Pep *knows* Barça, so has Klopp come to *know* Liverpool.

Klopp has long since become an honorary Scouser, so much so that in his resignation announcement, he promised, solemnly, and I take him at his word, that he would never manage another club in England.

Klopp knows what an order of betrayal that would be.

And so, like Pep, Klopp has come to know the cost of what it means to manage a football club who embodies the heart and soul of a people. And, make no mistake, to be a Scouser is to be in the world in a very distinct way. Speaking in an accent almost unintelligible to anyone but the locals, suspicious of the rest of the country in which they find themselves, prone to understanding themselves as the victims of Tory machinations (with good reason, I hasten to add), Liverpool and LFC fans are positioned at a searing remove from the world.

To be a Scouser, to commit oneself to LFC, is to know alienation. It is also to find solace, succor, and existential meaning in LFC. And, as such, it is to embrace this singular alienation.

Eventually, such a mode of being must exhaust even the most hardy of Scousers.

After nine years of giving himself so fully to the city and its people, to LFC partisans the world over, it became too much.

There will no doubt be moments when Klopp will miss it. He might even, like Bill Shankly did after resigning as manager in 1974, fifty years earlier, regret his decision.[26] Shankly sought to return, but by then, Paisley was in the job and the club's board was not going back on its decision.

Both Shankly and Klopp pronounced themselves tired, exhausted by the intensity of the job.

Both were men, managers of the people—of the people of the city of Liverpool. Shankly phrased that relation succinctly: "I am the people's man. Only the people matter." But there comes a time when the "people's man" has nothing left to give the people.

But the people never forget. And they are eternally grateful.

Maybe the people know how much it is they ask.

Maybe the people ask for so much because they themselves give everything they have to give. They give all that they have to Liverpool Football Club.

Sometimes they give their very lives. Ninety-seven of them did.

Kenny Dalglish knew, whether articulately or not, that no matter how much it is he (and Marina, his wife) gave in that time of traumatic loss, less was being asked of him than the people had showed themselves prepared to give—no, to sacrifice, and it was accidental self-sacrifice. Lives ended because they went to watch an FA Cup tie.

In European football, Liverpool and FC Barcelona make demands upon a manager that, arguably, no other club on the continent does.

Pep can go on. But only because Man City means less.

Liverpool means too much to Klopp.

Klopp means so much to Liverpool and its fans.

So much.

Pep had already experienced his Liverpool-means-too-much moment.

Though he was still a young man at forty-one years of age when he quit Barça in 2012, it was nevertheless too much for Pep.

Klopp will be fifty-seven when he takes his leave of Liverpool.

Full of passionate intensity.

But how are we to take the measure of years, all nine of them, in Scouser manager years?

All our metrics, we surely know, are insufficient. All our instruments for measuring time, scientifically imprecise as they already are, cannot begin to account for what it means to be in charge of the Scouser heart or the Catalan soul in every Premier League game, in every FA Cup tie, in every European encounter.

Multiply that by nine. And that's just the beginning.

Pep is Catalan to his marrow.

What it means to be a Scouser has seeped into Klopp's bones, as it did into Shankly's and Paisley's. It may have even reached the marrow; it surely has in Kenny's case. There is a reward, and a cost, to taking on the burden of "only the people matter" if you're the person on whom the people stake their lives.

Klopp, maybe even more than Shankly, knows what it feels like to have the love come flowing down from the stands, especially from the Kop End at the beginning of the match and then again when the game is over.

Klopp, I would venture, has gotten physically closer to Liverpool fans within the confines of the stadium than any other LFC manager.

His wife, Ulla Sandrock, has too.

In 2021, Liverpool plays Man City at the Etihad. At the end of the game, which ends in a draw, Klopp and Pep are talking. Pep inquires about where Klopp's wife sat during the game.

In the stands, with the LFC fans, Klopp tells him.

Pep is dumbfounded and asks if Klopp really is mad.

She's safe with them, Klopp tells Pep. They'll look after her.

Damn straight they will. And they, those loyal Scousers, did. They looked after her just fine.

Klopp can trust his wife to the LFC fans.

Alles gut.

January 31, 2024.

It is the second game in the countdown—Liverpool at home to Chelsea.

The final score is Liverpool 4, Chelsea 1.

It's almost a stroll.

Diogo Jota, a delightful striker, opens the scoring in the twenty-third minute.

I am a huge fan of Jota.

The Portuguese international is genuinely two-footed. He can strike the ball, with lethal precision, with both feet. Jota's former teammate, the Senegalese forward Sadio Mané, once commented that, after years of watching Jota in practice and in games, he still couldn't tell if Diogo was left- or right-footed. How about both, Dio?

At 5′7″, Jota is a monster in the air. He outjumps much taller central defenders. He passes with pinpoint accuracy. Plus, he is all action and is not afraid to put his foot in. I used to love watching Jota.

With Trent Alexander-Arnold injured, the twenty-year-old Northern Irish international Conor Bradley steps in with an otherworldly confidence. Firm in the tackle, marauding down the right wing, putting in crosses that bristle with intent, Bradley gets his name on the score sheet. It is his first senior goal for LFC, and Liverpool goes up 2–0 in the thirty-ninth minute.

In the sixty-fifth minute, Bradley hangs a cross perfectly that the young Hungarian captain Dominik Szoboszlai,[27] who plays in the midfield for LFC, duly nods home. It's now 3–0.

In the seventy-first minute, Chelsea pull one back, but Liverpool's Colombian striker Luis Diaz puts the contest to bed in the seventy-ninth minute with a neatly taken goal.

That's pretty much when I stop watching.

I don't make it to the end of the game.

I know I can't do this again.

I'm done—this time for good.

February 1, 2024.

I pick Nip up from school.
 "I've got bad news for you," I say.
 "What?" he demands.
 "It's about [Lewis] Hamilton."
 "What about Hamilton?" he presses.
 "He's leaving Mercedes next season."
 "Where's he going?"
 A frown descends upon my face. "You'll never guess."
 "Ferrari?" Nip guesses right. He's incredulous. He hates Ferrari. For Nip, this is a betrayal.
 We love Hamilton in his Mercedes livery.
 2024, Hamilton in the Mercedes Silver Arrow. One more go round.
 Then, Lewis will don the bright red of Ferrari's Prancing Horse.
 It'll take some getting used to.
 Had Klopp not announced his resignation, I'd never have known this, because I'd stopped following sport.
 I've got three or four Hamilton Mercedes baseball hats.
 I'll have to wear them to the point of wearing them out this year.
 What good will my Mercedes hat be next season?

1:10 p.m., February 6, 2024.

ILR is where it's happening.

"A statement win," says DJ Nix, a native son of North Carolina and sophomore guard on Brian Earl's team. Like any good North Carolina basketball player, DJ wears Michael Jordan's number, 23. For all that, DJ had the opportunity to play at Duke, but the recruiters were clear that he wouldn't get much time. This means that DJ, in his infinite wisdom, gave up the sunny South for gray, drab Ithaca.

I'm just leaving my class in Ives Hall, and DJ is walking in the opposite direction, on his way to class, when we run into each other.

"Congrats on the Harvard win," I offer, which prompts DJ's response. We fist bump.

And a signature win, it was.

After Cornell scraped by Dartmouth, the Battle of Ivy Colors continued. The night after the Big Green hosted the Big Red, the Big Red motored down to Cambridge, Massachusetts, to play the Harvard Crimson on Saturday, February 3, 2024.

It's a close game in the first half; the teams go into halftime with Cornell up by three, 38–35. But Cornell comes out strong in the second stanza, led by Zeke. With his seventeen points and six rebounds, Guy Ragland Jr.'s sixteen points and five boards, and AK's fifteen points (5-7 shooting), Cornell scores fifty-one points in the second half to put the game to bed, 89–76.

With this win, Cornell's 6–0 and tied for first in the Ivies with Yale.

Gone is the sloppiness of the previous night's game against Dartmouth; it has been replaced by poise and execution. The ball moves smartly, players make good decisions, and even with "Smooth Operator" out (a medial collateral ligament [MCL] injury), Cornell still manages to stretch the floor. Just as important, they play intense defense.

Everybody contributes. In the first half, DJ, Adam Tsang-Hinton (sophomore; pre-med, which impresses Zeke no end; me, no less so), and Beccles see time and all put in a shift.

This win should make Brian Earl and his coaching staff happy, especially with the big one on tap next Saturday, February 10, when Cornell travels to New Haven to take on the Yale Bulldogs in the battle of the unbeatens.

It should be quite a game.

January 31, 2024.

I'm on the couch, watching Liverpool play Chelsea in that Premier League game I just described.

Ezra comes home from school. He can't believe what he is seeing. I am watching an LFC game.

"Since when?" he asks, an inquiry at once arch and relieved in tone. I'm finally watching LFC again, something he didn't think he'd see.

"Since Klopp announced he's leaving," I reply.

Nip gets a little giddy.

"I'm glad that you're watching again," he says before heading to his room to do some gaming, no doubt. After that, Jane will take him to basketball practice, and I'll pick him up.

Jürgen Klopp's Birthday.

Jürgen Klopp was born on June 16, 1967.
 A historic day, June 16 is for me.
 I started high school in apartheid South Africa in January 1976.
 Five months into my high school career, the defining event of my youth took place.
 On the sixteenth of June in 1976, black students in Soweto, Johannesburg, protested the apartheid regime's decision to make black students receive much of their tertiary education in Afrikaans, the language of the regime, a language hated by the disenfranchised because of its association with the regime. (In South Africa, as in much of the rest of the world, the day comes before the month so it's the sixteenth of June, not June 16.)
 In response to the students' protest, the regime unleashed its repressive machinery, killing a student, Hector Pieterson, making his name synonymous with the event of Soweto.
 With that, the sixteenth of June was etched into the political memory of my generation of disenfranchised South Africans.
 It became the day when we, as high school students, took to the streets against the regime.
 Looking back now, it seems clear to me that the sixteenth of June 1976 might have been the beginning of the end for white minority rule in South Africa.
 Fourteen years later it would, officially, be over.
 I thus feel an affinity with Klopp. On his ninth birthday, I came of political age.
 Brian Earl was born in 1976.

1:00 P.M., February 8, 2024.

My class runs from 11:40 A.M. to 12:50 P.M., Tuesdays and Thursdays.

After the class ends, I'm talking to a couple of students when who should appear in the doorway: none other than Messrs. Williams and Boothby, on their way to class. They're just stopping in.

This is how I find out about "Smooth Operator's" MCL injury. "I'll be alright for Saturday," he assures me.

No longer a starter after having been one during the first half of the 2022–23 season, Boothby has responded well to coming off the bench. From my vantage point, I see him moving more, taking defenders—who fear his three-point shooting—with him, dragging them out of position. But he is also looking for his shots and, more often than not, making them. What is more, he is taking shots from more spots on the floor, whereas previously he seemed to favor the right-hand side of the key.

To me, "Smooth Operator" looks like a more relaxed player.

Nas, as he always does, asks about "E."

He commiserates about how bad Nip's team is but insists that Ezra just has to keep going.

Boothby murmurs his assent.

Deep down, I wonder if this is why I am so attached to this team; Nas, Zeke, Manon care about my son and always ask about him. So too does "Jiggy" (Beccles), who comes to his games, if only to secure nutritious snacks.

If nothing else comes from Ezra's basketball career, at least he has had the chance to be around a group of older players, Division I athletes, who show him how to be a considerate, thoughtful human being, one who should always be able to see others.

They are a group of funny, full-of-sh-t guys who work hard at their game. Zeke, Nas, "Smooth Operator," to say nothing of Chris Manon and every other member of the team, I suspect, each have their own brand of crazy. But what stands out to me in their interactions with Nip is that they are a bunch of guys who are not consumed by themselves. Or, if they are, they are entirely capable of stepping away from that mode of self-absorption when they're around kids. I've watched them at practice, when Brian Earl's boys, Dylan, Owen, and Cooper, are around. After games, the players engage Jon Jaques's daughter, Carina. I've seen Zeke and Chris with their little brothers. I've seen Nas, time after time, just goofing off with Zeke's and Chris's brothers and any other kids who happen to be around.

In this regard, Brian Earl leads the way. Whenever he and I talk, without fail, one of his first inquiries is "How's Ezra?"

That seems to be how Brian most often ends his texts.

Ulla Sandrock.

Liverpool fans owe Ulla Sandrock a huge debt.
 It was she who forbade her husband, Jürgen Klopp, from becoming the manager of our hated rival, Manchester United—not once, but twice.
 Ulla clearly knows what's good for Jürgen better than Jürgen does himself. *Vielen dank, Ulla.*
 Now and then, LFC earns its moniker, "The People's Club."
 Which Manchester United most certainly is not.

February 9, 2024.

Ezra doesn't get too much time in tonight's game, but he does stay true to form. He blocks a shot, again with his left hand, after which he is summarily taken out.

It's inexplicable, but he takes it in stride—or so it appears at first glance.

With two minutes and fifty-three seconds left in the game and IHS down by twenty-nine, Nip's in the game, the last conference game of the season, when the coach calls a time-out. He benches Nip, who is utterly dumbfounded by this decision. I'm sitting two rows back, and I watch Nip's face. An undisguisable "F-ck" issues forth.

He clearly is not taking this substitution in stride.

This decision, it beggars belief.

What's the coach thinking by putting the seniors, who have been nigh on useless, selfish, and allergic to defense all year, back in? (I should add, however, that there are a couple of exceptions; S. and T. have battled hard all season; S. is a gamer, and T. rebounds with gusto. T., however, does seem allergic to putting the ball in the net; offense appears not to be his thing.)

The IHS guards have SG: the Selfish Gene.

A violation for me, this abbreviation, SG.

In my world, those are the initials of Stevie Gerrard, a great Liverpool captain, perhaps the greatest.

Stevie G. was by no means a selfish player. He would do whatever it took to win. He would play in whatever position was needed to secure victory.

But here we are, in that moment when SG designates a tendency to do exactly the opposite of what one Steven George Gerrard did. The exact opposite of Stevie's mindset.

In place of commitment to the team, SG has come to stand for the Selfish Gene, where the individual stat line takes precedence. A stat line that can make its way, rapidly, onto social media.

As if everyone's forgotten Andy Warhol's time limit—fifteen minutes of fame, no more.

Twenty-nine down with less than three minutes to go; does the coach have a secret plan? Has he got IHS primed for a comeback? Does the coach have the opposition just where he wants them? Has he deliberately spotted them a twenty-nine-point lead?

Nip takes a seat, rightfully disgusted.

The inexplicability of the coach's decision is poetic—if by poetic, you mean the opening two lines of that famous Countee Cullen sonnet, "Yet Do I Marvel":

I doubt not God is good, well-meaning, kind,
And did He stoop to quibble could tell why[28]

Cullen's sonnet is about how unfathomable to the white world a black poet is—"Yet do I marvel at this curious thing: / To make a poet black and bid him sing!"[29] All I'm suggesting is that it would take the Romantic Bard of the Harlem Renaissance to explain yanking the players on the floor in favor of seniors, especially the guards, who have failed repeatedly this season—eighteen times, to be exact.

I doubt that the Romantic Bard of the Renaissance can explain this coaching inexplicability. It may be work best left to God himself.

All Nip can do is fume and swear. He is way past quibbling.

I have little hesitation in declaring Nip's coach a decent human being. But his coaching strategies have the effect of leaving me, and maybe a few others, wondering exactly what the hell is going on in his head when he makes decisions that seem to be either boneheaded or, worse, myopic; his vision of coaching only extends to giving seniors, who are woeful and devoid of work ethic, extended minutes, regardless of the state of the game.

Surely even the late Ray Charles can see that this is a lost cause—down twenty-nine with two minutes and fifty-three seconds left on the clock?

February 10, 2024.

These are the notes I took on the Cornell–Yale game.

The Yale coach, James Jones, is one of only two African American coaches in the men's Ivies. (The other is Tommy Amaker of Harvard.) Jones reminds me of the former Portland Trailblazer (and later, Houston Rockets) shooting guard, Clyde "The Glide" Drexler.

Like Drexler, Jones has a shaven head, and like Drexler's, Jones's chin angles forward. In Drexler's case, it is in an anticipatory merriment, whereas with Jones, it has more of a scholastic bearing, as befits a Yale man, one might say. Yale, after all, is the institution that gave us the style that we know as Ivy prep.

Jones is a dapper dresser. He is nattily attired in a suit. Everything beautifully coordinated, down to his striped socks.

When Cornell plays Yale at Newman Arena on February 23, they will have to do a better job of rebounding.

To my mind, that will be the difference. If Cornell matches Yale in rebounding, the game is theirs for the taking.

Cornell's best player, Chris Manon, is a better player than his Yale counterpart, Danny Wolf.

There will be extra incentive for Manon, Zeke, Boothby, and Hansen on the weekend of February 23 and 24. It will be their final home stand. This will be the last time they suit up as Cornell players at Newman Arena.

I'm hoping that they can go out with a bang.

But it will be tough. Jones's Yale Bulldogs will, I am sure, show themselves, once again, to be a formidable opponent.

Newman will have to be loud.

And Brian Earl's boys will have to give the Cornellians something to cheer about.

The Cornell fans will have to get on Yale in the same way that they rattled Princeton—especially in the way they got under the skin of Princeton's Lee.

They need a different chant but something as loud and disconcerting as the shouts of "Over-Rated" every time Lee touched the ball.

Cornell will have to make home court count.

For my part, I'm already dreading the prospect of saying goodbye to Manon, Boothby, Hansen, and Zeke.

I'm not sure I'm ready for it.

I can't imagine that they will quite know what's about to hit them that weekend, especially because February 24 will be Senior Night. That means all the seniors' families will be in attendance.

I'm expecting a night of raw emotion.

Jane's already remarked on my bringing up Senior Night repeatedly.

But once the game starts, that stuff will all be pushed to the back of their heads.

Surely, Earl and his staff will keep the team on track and focused.

February 11, 2024.

Mahomes Mystique.

Its Super Bowl Sunday. The Kansas City Chiefs (KC) are playing the San Francisco 49ers.

One of my oldest friends in the United States is a 49ers fan. The dad on one of Ezra's AAU basketball teams is a 49ers fan. In fact, M. is my favorite basketball dad. M. is that rare dad who is devoted to his son but sees every other kid on the team. M. is not myopic. He is not in the least parochial in his fandom.

I've got nothing against the Niners, but Patrick Mahomes, the KC quarterback, is one of my two favorite NFL players. The other is Justin Jefferson of the Minnesota Vikings.

Super Bowl LVII provides what many other Super Bowls do not: a competitive contest.

The 49ers dominate but can't convert territorial superiority and their superior time of possession into points.

At halftime, the Niners go in up 10–3.

I talk with my friend Cary Wolfe at halftime, and he says, wisely, "KC has the Niners exactly where they want them. KC has played terribly, and yet they're only down a score."

He's a smart man, Cary.

"I've enjoyed watching the Niners defense," Cary goes on.

It's hard to argue with that. The Niners defense, led by defensive coordinator Steve Wilks, has done a superb job denying Mahomes. KC's run game can't really get going; their passing game records only one big play in the entire first half, and even that big play is negated on the very next possession when KC fumbles.

In the third quarter, due to a muffed punt by the Niners, Mahomes and the KC offense finally manage to add to the measly three points they had on the board at halftime.

It's a tight game, with points at a premium.

Fittingly, the game goes to overtime with a tie score of 19–19.

The controversial moment will occupy pundits and fans for at least the week that follows the Super Bowl.

In overtime, the Niners win the toss and elect to receive the ball.

The conventional logic is that if you win the toss, you defer. You let the opposition have first go on offense.

Later, it turns out that Mahomes, the KC captain who lost the toss, could not believe what the Niners did. That is, he was ebullient at KC's good luck—and at the 49ers' inexplicable stupidity.

The Niners head coach, Kyle Shanahan, who did not inform his players in training camp about the new rules in the event of a Super Bowl overtime, does not go by the book.

The Niners receive the ball and duly kick a field goal.

This means that KC must, at the very least, match that to extend the game.

Of course, this also means that KC, with Mahomes under center, has effectively committed to giving themselves four downs on every possession.

The moment that the Niners can only manage a field goal, you know that it's game over.

This is Patrick Mahomes, already a two-time Super Bowl winner, that player who, the bigger the moment, the brighter the lights, the higher the stakes, is going to come out on top.

To no one's surprise, this is how the game ends—on a Mahomes touchdown.

Mahomes completes a short pass to Mecole Hardman, and it's Super Bowl number three for Mahomes and KC.

"Jackpot, Kansas City," sings Jim Nantz, the CBS commentator. On the money, is our Jim. You get the feeling, listening to Nantz, that he's been saving that one for just such a moment. After all, it could as easily have been "Jackpot, San Francisco." Nicely timed, Jim.

Nantz had been saving just that phrase in the hope that he'd be able to use it here, in Las Vegas, this being the first time that Vegas is hosting the Super Bowl.

Nantz was saving his killer line for the Mahomes Mystique.

Sorry, Niners quarterback Brock Purdy, who is praised by many commentators as a good game manager. You engineer long drives that result in field goals. You're a field goal specialist, Brock.

Manage that.

Why the Niners Made It Difficult to Root for Them.

First, the Niners organization has the feel of a good ole boy network—a white good ole boy network, to wit.

Their general manager, John Lynch, was a successful player in the NFL who won a Super Bowl ring with the Tampa Bay Buccaneers and played for the Denver Broncos. Lynch is a graduate of Stanford University, as is the Niners running back, Christian McCaffrey, son of Ed McCaffrey, former wide receiver on the Denver Broncos. Father and son, Stanford alums.

The Niners head coach, Kyle Shanahan, is the son of Mike Shanahan, former head coach of the Denver Broncos and the Washington Commanders—although the Washington team was still named the Redskins when Mike Shanahan coached the team. Mike Shanahan, who began his NFL coaching career as the offensive coordinator for the Niners, won two Super Bowls with the Broncos.

Kyle Shanahan was hired by Gary Kubiak of the Houston Texans as their wide receivers' coach.

In 2008, Kyle Shanahan became the youngest coordinator in the NFL, as he was named the Texans' offensive coordinator.

For the 2023 season, Klint Kubiak, son of our old friend Gary, was the offensive coordinator of the Niners.

The white good ole boy network has its tentacles in every NFL franchise, so singling out the Niners is, on the face of it, unfair. The Bill Belichick tree shows itself to have born equally odious fruit.

But, when we get to the Niners' recently fired defensive coordinator, Steve Wilks, maybe a different understanding may present itself—something not quite as savory.

Second, the hype around the Niners quarterback begins to stick in one's craw after a while.

The two hundred sixty-second and final pick of the 2022 NFL draft, Brock Purdy has defied the odds completely. Generally, the final pick of the draft is dismissed as "Mr. Irrelevant."

Not so with Purdy, who led the Niners to the NFC championship game in the 2022 season and to the Super Bowl a year later.

The Niners, to their credit, have surrounded Purdy with a remarkable array of talent: the tight end George Kittle, the running back McCaffrey, and wide receivers such as Deebo Samuel, Brandon Aiyuk, and Jauan Jennings, the latter of whom was superb against KC. The Niners' defense, first under the current Houston head coach DeMeco Ryans and this season under Wilks, is a star-studded roster.

Defensive linemen Arik Armstead and Nick Bosa and linebackers Dre Greenlaw and Fred Warner are just four of their defensive stars.

The 2023 edition of the 49ers boasted a roster, on both sides of the ball, with more than enough talent to win a Super Bowl—a stacked roster, as the saying goes.

All this talent is led by Purdy, who has the look of a frat boy cleaned up for his first on-campus job interview.

Purdy is lauded, as we have said, by many pundits as a good "game manager."

That is, he is smart, he makes good decisions, he "manages" the Niners offense efficiently. He makes "good reads"; he does not turn the ball over or force his throws.

He is smart.

That is, he is *not* a *black* quarterback.

That is, Purdy is not prone to making high-risk throws. By this NFL logic, that would make the Buffalo Bills white quarterback, Josh Allen, a supremely black quarterback. A real gunslinger, is Josh, as was Brett Favre. But white boys get a pass.

White quarterbacks are smart. Black quarterbacks are *athletic*—that is, they have great mobility, they have tremendous "instincts." But they're not cerebral. They are prone to making "bone-headed" decisions. They will cost you the game, a shot at the title.

How are we to understand Patrick Mahomes, then?

He won his two Super Bowls with KC playing all their playoff games at their home Arrowhead Stadium.

It must be home field advantage, then.

Well, apart from their first game against the Miami Dolphins in the 2023 playoffs, KC had to win their way to the Super Bowl on the road.

They played in Buffalo, against Josh Allen, a player for whom I have a real soft spot. He plays quarterback (QB) like a drunken cowboy, a fitting description for a player who grew up a farm boy in Firebaugh, California, and a graduate of the University of Wyoming Cowboys. Allen is fearless, intensely competitive, and wonderfully athletic.

They played in Baltimore, against the top-seeded Ravens—black QB Lamar Jackson against black QB Mahomes.

The Ravens have a fearsome defense.

Mahomes puts up seventeen points in the first half.

KC wins 17–10.

They go an entire half without points.

Can it be said that Mahomes "managed" the game well?

Or did he just manage to "win on the road"? Is it both, maybe?

Third, there is Travis Kelce.

If Josh Allen is a drunken cowboy, then the KC tight end is a raging bull in a bar full of inebriated steel workers.

But an eminently likeable bull, I should add, one who would charm those garrulous steel workers.

Kelce seems to play with a single intention: to knock over as many opponents as possible. Kelce relishes contact. And he does so with a smile—a broad, unrestrained smile. Kelce is loud and boisterous in victory, delightfully gracious in defeat.

And Travis Kelce has *that* effect on the spectator: you want to root for him.

There is nothing polished or refined or understated about Kelce.

Onto the podium, where the Lombardi Trophy had been handed over by the NFL commissioner and done its round with the KC brass, general manager, owner, coach Andy Reid, and MVP (again) Mahomes, steps Kelce, celebrating like he means it.

Deep from out of his core erupts a guttural Elvis invocation—the fat Vegas Elvis, the Elvis in the white jumpsuit, the hopped-up-on-something Elvis, not the slim, gyrating, part Cherokee kid from Memphis, or the "Love Me Tender" Elvis, or the side-burned, hip-swiveling, gravelly voiced Elvis made fit for public consumption by the shady Dutch entrepreneur Colonel Tom Parker.

Then come three guttural Travis Kelce eruptions:

"Viva, Las Vegas!"

"Viva, Las Vegas!"

"Viva, Las Vegas!"

Travis Kelce is so happy he makes you want to be happy for him. Such is the happiness he exudes. Such is his unfettered id. Kelce draws you into his orbit of manic joy.

I am so freaking happy for Travis Kelce.

Plus, he is dating—as the entire world knows—Taylor Swift. I, while no Swiftie, am a Taylor Swift fan. There's a world of difference between being a Swiftie—that is, a true believer in *Time Magazine*'s 2023 Person of the Year; those who follow her every move on social media, some of my students among them; those who worship at the altar of Her Swiftie Highness—and being a fan. I've only got a couple of Taylor Swift albums, *1989* and *Folklore*, both of which I like. Besides, how could anyone not warm to those melancholic, catchy lines from "Style." If you'll allow me some cultural latitude, Swift's "Style" is like Don McLean's "American Pie" for the Swiftie generation: "You got that James Dean daydream look in your eye."[30] A paean to nostalgia for a generation barely old enough to remember that moment when Abercrombie & Fitch was the governing aesthetic.

Doesn't the sense of loss that pervades Swift's "Style" just conjure up Edward Hopper's "Nighthawks"? It makes me want to take a walk down this Swiftie-paved Boulevard of Broken Dreams.

On June 13, 2024, Taylor Swift plays a concert at Anfield as part of her "Eras" world tour.

Jürgen Klopp returns to Anfield. Making of Klopp, by his account, "officially a Swiftie."[31]

An early birthday present to yourself, Jürgen, or was it a gift from Ulla?

Either way, you gotta love the circumstances under which Klopp makes his return to Anfield.

I just hope that Travis Kelce was in attendance. So that he could see what a real football stadium looks like. Arrowhead's not Anfield, Travis.

Plus, Travis Kelce put out an ad urging everyone to get vaccinated against COVID, unlike his more ideologically retrograde NFL brethren, such as the loathsome right-winger Aaron Rodgers, formerly quarterback for the Green Bay Packers and now plying his trade for the snake-bitten New York Jets.

In his first series in his first game under center for the Jets, Rodgers was sacked by Buffalo Bills linebacker Leonard Floyd, tearing the quarterback's achilles, thereby ending Rodgers's season.[32]

Like I said, a snake-bitten franchise.

Plus, Travis Kelce's brother, Jason, the recently retired center for the Philadelphia Eagles, is as unrestrained in his behavior as his brother. In the KC-Buffalo Bills game, when Travis scores a touchdown, Jason takes off his shirt—it's freezing in Buffalo—and throws himself on the mercy of the Bills fans.

Bills fans know crazy, so they—despite their impending loss—make sure that no harm comes to Jason.

Viva, Buffalo.

You get the feeling that there's no "Viva" anything in Brock Purdy.

Is Travis Kelce, temporarily, the blackest white man in America since Eminem?

Taylor Swift Puts the Fear of Electoral Defeat into MAGA.

The other reason I like Taylor Swift is that she scares the electoral crap out of the MAGA mob. In 2023, Swift encouraged her millions of followers to register to vote:

> On Tuesday morning, the singer posted a short message on Instagram encouraging her 272 million followers to register to vote. Afterward, the website she directed her fans to—the nonpartisan nonprofit Vote.org—recorded more than 35,000 registrations, according to the organization.[33]

What's not to like about this—the far right, the extreme right, the MAGA crazies getting their knickers in a twist because Taylor Swift has the social media clout to get people to exercise their democratic right?

In the days leading up to the Super Bowl, the likes of Vivek Ramaswamy were almost panting with concern that, should KC win, Swift would come out—publicly, this time—and endorse Joe Biden's reelection bid.[34] (Does anyone still remember who Vivek Ramaswamy is? Apologies for bringing back such smarmy, anodyne memories. And it wasn't just Ramaswamy. The right-wing internet was full of like-minded crazy Taylor Swift–related conspiracy theories.)

Swifties, on the other hand, had much more important matters on their hands. They wondered whether, should KC win, Travis Kelce would propose to Taylor.

To boot, Ramaswamy, Trump's Mini-Me, took this fear of Swift to enlist voters to its natural conspiratorial conclusion. KC was guaranteed to win the Super Bowl,[35] regardless of what the Niners did. The outcome was assured, not only because of Taylor Swift, but also because Patrick Mahomes is the NFL's poster boy. Officiating crews give Mahomes and KC special latitude, because Mahomes is the face of the NFL, and no one among the NFL's top brass wants to see Mahomes go down in defeat.

Oh, Tom Brady, how quickly they've forgotten you.

The funny bit here is that these conspiracy theories made the MAGA mob into Niners fans, unwitting or not, at least for the day of the Super Bowl.

Did this make the MAGA mob a bunch of bleeding-heart liberals whenever Patrick Mahomes plays? Or is it only on Super Bowl Sunday?

Or did the MAGA mob imagine that they could just sign on as Niners fellow travelers for a day?

Just so that we're on the same page here, we're talking about the San Francisco 49ers. San Francisco is the hometown of Nancy Pelosi, former Speaker of the House of Representatives, a Democrat, the scourge of Trump and his ilk. Remember how one of the MAGA mob took a mock dump on Speaker Pelosi's desk on January 6, 2021? San Francisco is also the city where the former Vice President (and presidential candidate) Kamala Harris served as district attorney? *That* San Francisco?

Do the January 6 insurrectionists prefer even their archnemesis in Congress, Nancy Pelosi, to Taylor Swift?

Is this the true measure of the Taylor Swift effect—that she can make Niners fans of the MAGA faithful? If so, she is a woman to be truly feared.

Whatever happened to that much vaunted conservative belief that states such as Missouri, Ohio, Kansas represent the American heartland, the true America? Don't they make up the Bible Belt, where good, God-fearing, white Americans are to be found? Aren't they the Bible Belters so despised by the coastal elites?

Lest we forget, KC's home games are played at Arrowhead Stadium, Kansas City, Missouri.

Patrick Mahomes plays for the Kansas City Chiefs. *Kansas City's team is still called the* Chiefs. *The NFL's Washington team is now named the* Commanders. *(Commanders in chief? Perfectly ironic, given how hapless the current Washington team is.*[36]*) No longer the* Redskins. *Took a while, but there you have it. Cleveland's Major League Baseball (MLB) team is now named the* Guardians. *Lame, I grant you, but the team is no longer the* Indians. *Atlanta's MLB team, unsurprisingly, is still called the* Braves. *Tomahawk chops are still a thing with the Atlanta fans.*

Imagine how Chiefs *and* Braves *sits with the indigenous communities in Missouri and Georgia, just for starters. Communities that have long opposed* *these names and have organized to have them changed.*³⁷ *Communities that continue to call for these franchises to do right by them. To understand the obvious historical reasons why these names give offense. Why their franchise mascots, emblazoned on their merchandise, constitute an affront to those communities that have for centuries endured the violence of the American settler colonial project.*

Why they have every right to demand that Atlanta and Kansas City change their team names. Replace the symbols on their baseball uniform (Atlanta).

Does this make KC fans dyed-in-the-wool Democrats?

Whatever is the matter with Kansas City?

It is not, clearly, President Joe Biden or Vice President Kamala Harris that the MAGA mob, the Proud Boy insurrectionists, and their marauding cousins, the Capitol rioters, fear. No, it's Taylor Swift and her millions of social media followers.

Who said popular culture doesn't matter?

Let all those who fear the return of violent MAGA rule hitch their wagon to Taylor Swift, who has made Kansas City, Missouri, the symbol of political resistance to all the America First types.

Let all those who believe in science side with Travis Kelce.

Does that make all New York Jets fans vaccine deniers? Incipient or practicing Republicans?

Viva Taylor and Travis! This pop culture power couple may be all that can save us from the MAGA monsters.

Travis Kelce, sadly for Swifties, did not propose.

*Maybe at next year's Super Bowl.*³⁸

The Morning After the Morning After the Morning After, the Niners Make You Happy They Lost.

Three days after the Super Bowl, Kyle Shanahan announces that he has decided to fire Steve Wilks.

He does this after having promised, just the day before, that "all his staff would be back."

Then, apparently, Kyle Shanahan "slept on it." What did Kyle Shanahan see in his sleep? What demons visited him? Were they black or white? How is it that Shanahan didn't see himself as the architect of his own nightmare?

Kyle Shanahan, praised by many NFL insiders as an "offensive genius," put up nineteen points against KC in regulation, three in overtime.

Kyle Shanahan's offense, which had to settle for field goals when touchdowns, in the first half, would have put the game out of KC's reach, walks away from a Super Bowl defeat without a scratch.

Made the dumb decision to receive the kickoff.

Kyle Shanahan's job is safe.

Klint Kubiak, offensive coordinator, leaves the Niners for the same position with the New Orleans Saints.

In the NFL, Shanahan, Kubiak, and their ilk are what passes for coaching "pedigree."

As if to the manner born.

Born with a silver coaching spoon in their mouths.

Who would bet against a third generation of Shanahans and Kubiaks patrolling an NFL sideline?

Not me.

Steve Wilks gets fired. The black defensive coordinator gets the boot.

Six games into the 2022 NFL season, the Carolina Panthers fire their head coach, Matt Rhule, fruit of the Belichick coaching tree—like Matt Patricia, Josh McDaniels, Joe Judge... Wilks, a North Carolina native, takes over, leads the team to a 6–6 record. Gets passed over for Frank Reich, a white coach, who duly bombs.[39]

Raheem Morris served three seasons as the head coach of the Tampa Bay Buccaneers. In 2012, he was fired. In 2024, Morris was recently hired as head coach of the Atlanta Falcons. Kevin Demoff, president of the Los Angeles Rams, remembers the hard truth that Morris spelled out to him after Demoff was sure that Morris would get another shot at a head coaching position. "Kevin, people like me don't get second chances."[40] Rare among black head coaches, Morris now has his second chance. Even if it took thirteen years.

Steve Wilks gave up nineteen points to Mahomes.

Nineteen.

To Mahomes.

Mahomes, together with Joe Montana (Niners) and Tom Brady (New England Patriots), the greatest QB of all time.

Nineteen.

In Super Bowl LIV, Mahomes scored thirty-one points against Shanahan's Niners—KC won 31–20.

In Super Bowl LVII, Mahomes put up thirty-eight points against the Eagles—KC won a tight one, 38–35.

The arithmetic is unarguable. When facing a defensive coordinator not named Wilks, Mahomes is averaging 34.5 points per Super Bowl win. Wilks pretty much halved that. With one of his defensive stars lost in the second quarter.

Wilks lost Dre Greenlaw, who suffered an unfortunate injury. Greenlaw was just running onto the field with nine minutes and twenty-six seconds left in the second quarter when the injury occurred. Wilks's defense still contained Mahomes, insofar as anyone can contain Mahomes.

Steve Wilks restricted Mahomes to field goals.

Steve Wilks kept the score to 10–3 in the first half. The Niners were in the lead.

Steve Wilks made KC punt on its first two possessions the third quarter.

KC only scored their first touchdown because of a muffed punt by the Niners' special team.

Steve Wilks's fate puts me in mind of how it is the Niners treated Colin Kaepernick.

Don't kneel.

In San Francisco, the song remains indelibly the same.

You dare not give up nineteen points to Patrick Mahomes.

Maybe we shouldn't be surprised. After all, the Niners franchise dedicated itself to an institutional whitening with its move from San Francisco to Silicon Valley—this at a moment in the city's history that is marked by the racial and ethnic cleansing of black people from San Francisco.[41]

This makes you side with Shannon Sharpe, the former NFL tight end who won Super Bowl rings with Green Bay (Brett Favre) and the Baltimore Ravens (Trent Dilfer, a game manager if there ever was one) and who can barely disguise his animus for Purdy.

Sharpe has no doubt as to why Purdy collects the plaudits. Sharpe knows, as surely as his name is Shannon Sharpe, why Wilks was canned.[42]

Purdy's reputed skill as a "game manager" is a racialized code discernible to everybody.

On the CBS postgame show, the African American host James Brown verbalizes the extent to which the Purdy-is-a-game-manager logic has permeated the world of the NFL.

With his (losing) performance in the Super Bowl, Brown says, Purdy has just elevated himself from "manager to executive."

I keep wondering what the *real* James Brown would have said.

"I don't feel good."

Whatever could be next? Brock Purdy, chief executive officer? Brock Purdy: CEO. It's a matter of time before Purdy's next promotion. Watch this space.

The hype around Purdy sticks in Sharpe's craw, as it does in mine.

Kyle Shanahan has the backing of a Niners franchise that fired a defensive coordinator who was, for a minimum of three quarters, outstanding and who didn't make the decision to receive the ball.

What neutral can root for the Niners after this?

Kyle Shanahan just lost his third Super Bowl after leading by ten points. What does Shanahan need to win a Super Bowl—a lead of eleven?[43]

How many more chances will Shanahan get?

Because, have no doubt, Shanahan's failures with the Niners will not prevent him from getting another head coaching job in the NFL when the Niners are finally tired of losing in the NFC championship game or in the Super Bowl. General Manager John Lynch too will tire of defeat.

And he won't have to wait thirteen years.

No matter, it is surely a matter of time before the next generation of McCaffreys suits up for Stanford and then gets drafted into the NFL before securing a trade to the Niners.

This is a little like the story that Buddy Ryan's son, Rex, likes to tell. Buddy Ryan was an innovative defensive coach. He worked on three teams that went to the Super Bowl—the Jets, the Minnesota Vikings, and the Chicago Bears, who won him a ring in Super Bowl XX in 1985. After this, Buddy had stints as head coach of the Philadelphia Eagles and the Arizona Cardinals, with a stint as Houston Oilers defensive coordinator sandwiched in between. According to Rex, who was a head coach at both the Jets and the Bills, he and his (fraternal) twin brother, Rob, had to work twice as hard under their father's tutelage. Rob got his start with Buddy at the Cardinals. Rob won Super Bowls with the New England Patriots (linebackers coach). He has been defensive coordinator for the Cleveland Browns and the New Orleans Saints, serving in the same capacity for, you've guessed it, his brother with the Bills.

One is thus tempted to quote Shakespeare to Rex Ryan: "The fraternal twin doth protest too much."

We don't know how many more chances Shanahan will get, but we know why he'll get them.

Rooney Rule or no Rooney Rule.

The Rooney Rule is bleached into NFL insignificance by the Ryan Rule, the Shanahan Rule, the Kubiak Rule.

Kyle Shanahan and Klint Kubiak, we should remember, have "NFL pedigree."

Thus, Shanahan is free to choke all he wants in the big games. He has before, and we know he will again.

After Shanahan's offensive genius and Purdy's game management come to naught, there can be no more black agnostics in the Super Bowl when the Niners are playing.

Had a black head coach in the NFL failed to explain the overtime rules to his players in preseason, as Shanahan so pointedly did not, the outcry would have been huge.

A black head coach not reminding his players of the rules in the Super Bowl? With a ring on the line?

Fuhgeddaboudit.

Double standard? Racism in the NFL? Surely not.

The criticism would have been intense. Black head coaches do not do their due diligence. They neglect their duties; they pay scant regard to the rules. These black head coaches do not prepare their players properly. They fail to inform them of something as basic as rule changes.

In other words, they could learn a thing or two about game management from Brock Purdy. Black head coaches are given to overlooking the "little things."

In short, blacks are really not cut out to be head coaches. They just don't have what it takes. They lack the mental acuity. It's not in their DNA. The minutiae is, unfortunately, what always escapes their attention.

Surely, by this logic, that makes Kyle Shanahan a black head coach?

You could have fooled me.

My dream scenario would be head coach Steve Wilks winning a Super Bowl against Kyle Shanahan after Shanahan's blown a twelve-point lead.[44]

Such an outcome might convince me that even if God is dead, the sharp end of poetic justice is not.

Better still, the Sharpe end of athletic justice is alive and well.

The long and the short of it, though, is much less a matter for mirth.

Kyle Shanahan kept his job and, with it, the power to fire Steve Wilks.[45]

CK, KC: As a Curse.

The Chicago Cubs, as every baseball fan knows, are reputed to have been cursed because, in 1945, during Game Four of the World Series, they ejected the pet goat of William Sianis, owner of the Billy Goat Tavern.

The Cubs, legend has it, would never win another World Series until they allowed the goat back into Wrigley Field.

The Cubs did win a World Series, in 2016, to the utter delight of my in-laws, Peg and the late Ron Juffer.

Have the San Francisco 49ers been cursed by how it is they treated Colin Kaepernick?

How does a franchise make right with history after ending the career of a black quarterback because he took a knee during the singing of the national anthem?

Are the Niners now under the bad-luck spell of CK—Colin Kaepernick? Or should that be KC—the Kaepernick Curse?

Damn, those two consonants, *K* and *C*, are sure playing havoc with San Francisco. Does KC stand first for Kansas City and then Colin Kaepernick, or is it the other way around? Either way, it's *K* and *C*.

I find it difficult to believe that the NFL gods, whom I'm convinced are red-baiting, right-wing conservatives, would have such a completely out-of-character sense of historical irony, but if this is their doing, this Curse, then fair play to them.

Maybe we should spell this curse with a *K*—as in *Kurse*.

February 16, 2024.

There's a scheduling conflict. Cornell has a 6:00 P.M. tip-off against Harvard tonight. Nip's coach has organized a nonconference game against nearby Trumansburg at 7:15 P.M. In the scheme of things, the IHS game against "T-Burg," a local rival that plays in a lower division, is meaningless. The IHS conference season ended last week in yet another defeat—a 2–18 season.

The good thing about this postseason game that is not a postseason game is that our older son, Alex, who lives just outside Minneapolis, is visiting. Alex will get in on Friday evening in time to see his brother play.

It does mean we'll have to stream the Harvard game. With an earlier tip-off, we'll be able to see most of the first half before leaving for Trumansburg.

Cornell starts off well. I'm glad to see the shooting guard, Cooper Noard, make shots again. It has been something of a lean spell for him, so when he hits his first shot, a three—trademark Cooper Noard—it is easy to feel good for him.

Noard and Manon score eleven each, and Nas leads the Big Red with fourteen.

Cornell wins 75–62.

That's win number seven, matching Cornell's Ivy win total for the 2022–23 season.

In the same fixture last year, Harvard beat Cornell.

With three more home games—Dartmouth tomorrow night, then Yale and Brown the weekend after—Cornell has a shot at the Ivy championship.

But I'm not going to jinx it.

Ezra doesn't get to play in the first half of the T-Burg game, and we're worried that he won't get in for half number two.

But, if Nip's not in, I can give almost my full attention to the Cornell game. "Up 3 at the half," I report to Jane.

"Up 10," late in the second half.

But Nip does get in, and with his first offensive possession, he drains a long two. Were it not for his foot on the line, it would have been a three, nothing but net.

Jane throws up her arms and whoops.

Later she confesses to me, "I thought he was going to airball it."

Later Nip confesses, "I thought I'd overshot it."

Overshoot all you want, kid, long as you produce the same result.

Big brother Alex is suitably impressed. It was worth the trip from Minneapolis.

Old and battered Knick fan that I am, nothing but net means only one thing—"Kiki VanDeWeghe, Baby." *Nothing but net*, that's what Patrick Ewing used to say about VanDeWeghe's step-back jumper. VanDeWeghe joined the Knicks (1989–92) from the Portland Trailblazers (1984–89), but he is best remembered as an All-Star during his time with the Denver Nuggets (1980–84). A star at UCLA before coming to the NBA, Kiki must have had a mortal fear of iron. When Kiki was on, his shots never touched the rim.

Nip hits three out of his four free throws, the only time he touches iron on a shot.

IHS wins. Alex got to see his little brother play. The fraternal bond has been strengthened.

On the way home, Alex and Nip dissect the game in detail.

Alex has a sharp eye, and he praises his brother and points out his shortcomings with the kind of directness that only a big brother can.

"Ferret."

Jane, Alex, and I are watching Ezra in Trumansburg.

I am suddenly struck by just how foreign this all is to me.

Our entire family, our daughter, Andrea, apart (she is, appropriately, in Cape Town at just that moment), is in attendance to watch our fifteen-year-old son/brother play in a game.

It was so different for me growing up in Cape Town, playing football in winter, cricket in summer.

I played sports to get away from my parents. My teammates and I used to walk from our home in Hanover Park, a working-class Cape Town neighborhood, to Rosmead Sports Ground, in Kenilworth, to play football. (Rosmead doubled as a cricket venue in spring and summer.) It was a distance of three and a half miles each way.

Sports freed us to do our own thing. They took up most of Saturdays. We left home around 8:00 or 8:30 A.M., got to Rosmead around 9:30 A.M. or so. We'd try to sneak into the grounds without paying. Sometimes we'd get caught, meaning we'd have to pay and then get a talking to from one of the officials there. After our game was done, we'd hang around to watch other games and get home somewhere around 5:00 or 6:00 P.M.

Our entire day was spent without parental supervision.

In the United States, families decamp en masse to watch their son or daughter compete.

Our household is no different.

In fact, in Cape Town, it always seemed to me that the occasional parent who did come to watch their kid play was either bored or, worse, obnoxious.

Maybe the obnoxious bit derives from just one such encounter I had as a player—an encounter that sticks in my head.

It's a Saturday in late May 1976. I'm captaining the Stephanians United (Stephs) under-fourteen team against Lilies. The game is being played on the Rosmead A pitch. (There are three other pitches, B–D.)

Lilies is a club based less than sixty yards from my front door in Hanover Park. It is headquartered in an apartment (*flat*, in South African terms) about seven or eight seconds away.

My Stephs team is up 2–0. I intercept the ball on our side of the halfway line, down the right flank. Because I've read the pass, I'm able to beat one player because his weight is going the wrong way, and then, in stride, I'm able to go by a second one—rare for me, as I'm no dribbler. As I pass the second Lilies player, he trips me. I throw up my hands, appealing for a foul. The ref duly obliges.

As the ref blows his whistle, one of the Lilies parents, standing less than a meter from me, yells directly at me while I'm still on my knees, in Afrikaans: "*Jy's niks werd nie, Farred.*" I can see the intensity and the dislike—for me, for the score, for the team I represent—in his eyes.

Except my name comes out as *Ferret*. I'll allow the mispronunciation of my last name; *Farred* is not an easy name for the Afrikaans tongue.

"You're not worth anything, Farred." That's what he's just said to me.

I dust myself off, place the ball, and give the Lilies parent the most scathing look my adolescent self can muster.

How do you like them apples?

We win the game.

Even today, I can picture that parent: short, balding, the few strains in the middle of his head swept determinedly back, held there by some hair gel that glistens on his scalp, bristling sideburns, dark eyes aimed directly at me. Without a doubt, that parent would have had his hair slicked back with Brylcreem, a brand popular among men of his generation in that era.

This adult lives within shouting distance of me. There's no way I'm telling my parents about this incident. His flat and my house are separated by a matter of meters. When he walks to catch the bus to go to work in the morning, he has to pass by our house.

We'll pass each other in the street, maybe as soon as tomorrow or Monday morning, when he goes to work and I go to school. An encounter is inevitable.

My look after I got fouled is designed to convey three things to him: I'm not afraid of him; my team is up and we're about to win the game, so he can say what he wants; and, as the kids say, I'll handle my own sh-t. That's the responsibility that comes with being allowed to walk from Hanover Park to Rosmead by myself.

I played football for twenty-two years. We went up against Lilies many a time and never lost to them—never.

In my final season, 1992, playing first team for Lansur United, we're down 0–3 against them.

Our central defender and my best mate on the team, Wakes Duncan, is hung over, leading to two of the three Lilies' goals, which are scored in quick succession.

Wakes's older brother, Hamat, is playing alongside him in central defense. Hamat is furious with Wakes and calls for the coach to sub him. Wakes is duly called to the bench.

Still and all, we come back and win the game, 5–3. We took your number a long time ago, Lilies.

These are different worlds, I know. In the United States, at a youth sports contest, any parent who said what that guy said to me would be summarily removed.

In the United States, at a youth sports contest, all spectators are asked to only applaud. The message, unfailingly, is "Be positive."

How about saying something negative to secure a positive outcome?

All of this can be reduced to, in a nutshell, the idea that you may praise the kid to the high heavens, if you please, but under no circumstances can you point out the kid's failures.

Kid can, say, turn the ball over eight times in thirteen possessions, frustrating his teammates to no end, driving spectators to distraction. But hey, no calling the kid to account. Instead, the common wisdom insists that we should all take a deep breath and find something positive to say. Platitudes abound. Take your pick from among the following:

"It's only a game."

"It's not about winning or losing. It's about playing the game."

Bill Shankly's most famous aphorism, I remind you: Football is not a matter of life or death. It's much more important than that.

"Hustle" is the all-purpose American sports invocation: "hustle," a cry that has a tendency to go up as the minutes on the clock tick down and the game is obviously lost; "hustle," that's the sound of hopelessness or desperation. Whatever you do, don't mistake it for strategic advice.

"Never mind, you'll get them next time."

You might very well get them next time. But not unless you fix what's wrong. Keep those turnovers to a minimum, that right there will improve your chances exponentially. Not unless you actually take the time to process that it was your poor point guard play that cost your team. Allow the adults who have a kid on your team to say that. About your kid. Why would you encourage your kid to be a selfish ball hog? Seriously, you're going to praise that?

Let the spectators call out a player's selfishness. Let the kids learn the necessary lesson of being criticized for their mistakes. Or, let them be smack-talked to by adults whose kid is on the opposing side. Let them grow the f-ck up by being held accountable for their failures. Regardless of their ambitions, or especially because of their ambitions, unfulfillable as they will most likely show themselves to be.

If you keep playing the way you played when you turned the ball over eight times in thirteen possessions, you'll just be ensuring that your team continues to lose.

In that way, make Bill Shankly your go-to guy. Football is not a matter of life or death. It's the most important way you can learn how to be in the world. That is, as a kid, you are not constantly deserving of praise. As an athlete, you'd better learn resilience, you'd better learn to take criticism. Because if you don't, that grand ambition of playing college basketball at Duke or UNC Chapel Hill is just a pipe dream. Find yourself at the Dean Dome playing for Duke against UNC, you'd better believe those Tar Heel fans are coming after you. And if you can't handle it, they'll let you know it in no uncertain terms. There'll be some choice language, too.

This is why parents should not, as a rule, coach their own kids.

Make that AAU Rule #1. No parent can coach a team on which their own kid is playing.

Or, worse, kids.

Father coaches are the bane of American youth sports.

Either these fathers are too tough on their kids, or they are too lenient.

When they're too tough, it can easily cross over into something that is perilously close to abuse. Watching Ezra in Stoughton, a suburb just outside of Boston, in July at the Dana Barros Basketball Club, I saw the coach of Barros's elite under-fifteen put his right hand on his son's throat. When Jane, another parent, and I erupted in protest, the player's mother yelled at us to mind our own business. "It's his son," she said emphatically. Guess that makes it alright.[46]

Either way, their kid gets special treatment, regardless of their protestations about treating every member of the team fairly. This especially happens when they insist that everyone on the team will be treated the same. That's just hogwash. Their kid will behave badly, they'll feign disapproval, and then they'll find an excuse for their kid not to be punished. Just make sure it's not your kid, because your kid will be punished to the fullest extent. If your kid is as talented as theirs, you know who will get the call come crunch time. That's how nepotism rolls.

Nepotism is Tefloned against shame or embarrassment.

Fathers coach their kids with an explicit design—to advance their kids' career, as we've established.

In the process, they create a cesspool of nepotism.

When their sons reach their high-water marks, the coaches, who have now reached their natural limit, try to inveigle their way into positions of ever-greater authority so as to continue their sons' advancement.

Their kid moves up from junior varsity (JV) to varsity? The father gives up his role as JV coach so that he can continue to call the shots.

The only thing that is as bad as a nepotistic small-town high school coach, varsity or JV, is a drunk-with-power little-town athletic director.

The smaller the pond, the greater the lust for absolute authority.

It's a sort of perverse take on the Peter Principle: promote your kid to the highest level that you can, and then, when the kid reaches his talent threshold, he stands exposed before the world. No longer afforded special treatment, his limitations as a player—whether they are due to a lack of innate skill, a lack of height, or simply a lack of athleticism—become evident, and the kid finds himself overmatched.

Tragic? I'm not so sure.

A form of the universe meting out justice? Maybe.

The universe compensating, belatedly, for the poor treatment suffered by those other kids who did not get a fair shake. Sounds plausible.

But what about the kid, that coach's son, who now finds himself out of his depth?

You feel for him. Like I feel for that kid from the Barros club. Maybe as much as I feel for those other kids.

Once installed, nepotism reveals itself in all its unfairness and ugliness.

The coach advances his kid *at the expense of the other players.*

There is no way to sugarcoat that effect. Nepotism denies other players a fair shot.

In small-town America, it is on display for all to see.

And every one of the players feeling the deleterious effects of this cesspool of nepotism is afraid to draw attention to this blatant unfairness. For good reason, they tell themselves. There will be a cost to play (less playing time, etc.).

The parents of these players are afraid to say anything because it means that their kid will be at a disadvantage.

As if the kid isn't already feeling the sharp end of nepotism.

It is a risk to speak out, to be sure. But isn't there also an upside?

Your kid gets to see you stand up for something that's right.

I know that here I run the risk of contradiction, given my position on letting kids handle their own sh-t.

But since that ship's already sailed, come on, in the name of all that is holy, don't tolerate this sh-t.

Don't imagine that you and your kid are not contaminated by swimming in the cesspool of nepotism.

If your kid is genuinely talented, he or she stands a better than even chance of making it. If the kid's only moderately talented, at least they've learned that nepotism is a social ill that should be resisted, no matter the costs.

Speaking out against nepotism might, or might not, make you, according to your calculus, a martyr.

In my book, speaking out against it just makes you a decent human being.

Not speaking out against it is far worse. It makes you complicit.

The choice is yours.

I am clear as to what my thirteen-year-old self would advise you.

I owe that kid, brash lad that he was—maybe even a little rash. But if you don't believe that kid, allow me to conscript U2's Bono to do the honors: "Don't let the bastards grind you down."[47]

You can't *wish* an end to nepotism.

You actually have to do something to bring about its unsightly demise.

That is, you have to *say* something about it, for your kid's sake.

Think of it as self-interest with a huge side of community spirit.

The way I see it, there are only two choices if you want to redress the situation.

First, wait out the nepotistic coach. That way, you invest your hope in anticipation of nepotism being the root cause of a losing season. For your purposes, the more catastrophic the season, the better. No one wants, you should argue, another losing season.

There is, however, a real downside to that, with no upside for your kid: an entire season will have been lost.

Second, speak up *before* the season starts.

Don't suffer in silence. Don't mutter darkly to yourself. Don't mutter darkly among your disgruntled selves, you ticked-off parents.

Just say out loud, where the coach can hear: *This is not right.*

The odds are against you, but would you really prefer that your kid endure a long season of pointless losing?

Come on, this is still America, land of the brave, home of the free.

Speak now or forever hold your anti-nepotistic peace.

February 17, 2024.

Dartmouth, again. Alex's first Cornell basketball game.

The Big Green are 1–7, bottom of the Ivy table (with Penn), but it's never a "gimme" game for Cornell.

And sure enough, midway through the first half, Dartmouth makes a run.

The Big Green take a fourteen-point lead.

But, led by Manon (who finishes with a massively efficient twenty-five points in twenty-six minutes; Chris was in foul trouble early and ended with four fouls), Cornell goes on a run of its own and goes into the break ahead, 50–47.

From that point on, the Big Red never look back. Cornell wins 89–80, with key contributions from AK Okereke (twelve points in twenty-two minutes) and Nas (fourteen in a team-high thirty minutes, to go with his five rebounds). Cooper Noard kicks in with eight (one for four on threes), and "Smooth Operator" knocks down a couple of three-pointers (on 2–6 shooting). However, the player who catches the eye tonight is the freshman guard from Wilmette, Illinois, Jake Fiegen.

Alex is impressed with Fiegen, considers him the best Cornell player after Manon.

Fiegen's stats are not Manonesque, but they are impressive—fourteen points in twenty-four minutes. Shooting 50 percent from beyond the arc (2–4), Fiegen shoots 6–9 overall to go with four rebounds. Only Nas has more rebounds.

In addition, Fiegen is a busy presence on defense, and he seems, for the second night in a row, ready to step up, freshman though he is.

Suburban boy though he is, Jake Fiegen plays like a black kid from the South Side of Chicago. Kid like Fiegen can only have one nickname, and his teammates are on it. I'll let you guess, but it begins with an "F" and it ends in an "O."

Next season, Cornell will lose four key seniors—Zeke, Hansen, Manon, and Boothby—but with this season's juniors, Nas and Ragland, sophomores AK and Noard, and the likes of Fiegen and Beccles, Brian Earl and Jon Jaques will have a solid squad to compete with next season.[48] That's not even accounting for what Adam Tsang-Hinton and the currently injured Josh Baldwin, among others, might bring to the table.

Just thinking this shows that I may already be deeper into this thing than I ever thought I'd be or maybe even wanted to be. I just wanted to root for Zeke, Manon, Hansen, Nas . . .

But there's a lot to play for this season—8-1 after the win tonight, with a shot at ending the night joint-top of the Ivies.

For that to happen, Princeton has to beat Yale.

8:00 p.m., February 17, 2024.

Maybe that was the final nail in the coffin—the moment I went home from Newman Arena knowing that I was going to stream the Yale at Princeton game.

It was game over, for me.

I knew that I was going to watch for a Yale loss.

And, thankfully, I got it.

On the Carril Floor at Jadwin Gym, undefeated Yale goes down to Princeton. The final score is 73–62, but there was a moment when things, from my point of view, got really hairy. Princeton went into the half ahead, 38–30.

But Yale, that bulldog with no quit in it, was not going to go quietly.

They chipped away, and for stretches, Princeton kept them at bay, but Yale kept plugging away; at one moment in the game, Yale pulled to within two points.

But Yale can't get over the hump, and by the end, Yale seems to have run out of steam. Yale's main guy, their center, Danny Wolf, struggles on offense for the entire game, netting exactly zero points. But Wolf does grab a team-high nine rebounds.

I just hope that Wolf isn't saving his offensive output for Newman Arena in six days. With Yale losing, and with Cornell's superior overall record (19-4 as compared to 17-7), Cornell ends the evening on top of the Ivy League standings.

It could all come down to the Yale–Cornell game on February 23.

It is a game that Cornell has to win.

Not only will a victory take them one win clear of Yale, but, with a trip to Princeton in the offing, it would be better to go to Jadwin ahead in the Ivies.
   Princeton's record is 7–2.
   It is just one win behind the leading two. There are five games to go. This coming weekend is Cornell's last home stand against Yale and Brown. After that, it's Penn, Princeton, and Columbia, all on the road.
   Yale goes to New York City after Ithaca this coming weekend, and they finish up at home against Dartmouth, Harvard, and Brown. Yale has the advantage, the neutral might say. Yale is a good team, but they're especially tough at home. Cornell might need Harvard to do them a favor.

5:34 p.m., February 18, 2024.

Jane, Alex, Nip, and I are having ice cream at Purity's, a local parlor in Ithaca, courtesy of the Cornell men's basketball team. The deal with Purity was that if Cornell scored seventy points, every fan in attendance would receive a voucher for a free scoop of ice cream.

In walks Mr. Jaques, his son, Micah, in his car seat.

Mr. Jaques, Micah, and I head to where Mr. Jaques's wife and daughter are sitting. I confess that I went home after the Cornell win and watched the Princeton–Yale game.

"Me too," says Mr. Jaques.

"Sicko," he remarks with his trademark self-deprecation.

You, Mr. Jaques? A sicko?

No, that's sort of in your job description—scout the opposition.

Prepare for the Penn–Princeton trip.

You're perfectly healthy, Mr. Jaques.

I'm the real sicko here.

But thanks for trying to make me feel better, if only unintentionally.

Our family's weekend, I kid myself, has been bookended by basketball.

No, our weekend has been organized and lived entirely around basketball—Cornell basketball.

How, in the good Lord's name, did this happen?

Phil Collins.

When you reach for the Phil Collins, that's when you know you're in deep trouble. "In too deep"—that's the Phil Collins line. It's Phil Collins at his best, with lines that stick in your head because they have, despite how saccharine it is, a "hook." Once you remember them, it takes days to dislodge them.

This is the musical violence that Zeke and his teammates have done to me: they've taken me back to my Phil Collins days, the unforgettable 1980s.

I'm trying to understand how things came to such a pretty pass.

It turns out it's not difficult at all.

After trying to tell myself that I supported the Cornell basketball team in 2010, I pull myself up short. That is decidedly not true.

This truth cannot even stand when I tell myself that Jane and I took Ezra, as a toddler, to watch a Cornell game.

We didn't really go to watch the Cornell team.

We went to watch Jon Jaques.

We followed Jon Jaques, especially when he was draining threes in the NCAA tournament in 2010.

We introduced Jon Jaques to my father-in-law, Ron Juffer, a man who played basketball into his eighties and a lifelong scholar of the game.

We made Jon Jaques, unbeknownst to him, a household name in Orange City, Iowa. But that was it. Jon Jaques was the beginning and end of our Cornell men's basketball fandom.

And that was only because in the previous semester, fall 2009, Mr. Jaques had been a student in my class on sport and literature—a really good student, too.

Jon Jaques showed himself to be a more than capable writer.

More than that, Mr. Jaques revealed himself to be a fundamentally decent human being.

When the class started, I had no idea as to who Mr. Jaques was, although, from his towering height of 6'6", I could guess that he might be a basketball player.

As the semester unfolded, the details slowly seeped out, and I became aware that Mr. Jaques was a co-captain of the Cornell men's team.

Mr. Jaques blogged about the team for *The New York Times*.

It made sense, as the kid could write. He probably still can, should the need arise.

And then came the revelation that got me hooked.

Jon Jaques was the co-captain of a team on which he did *not* start.

But his demeanor betrayed none of that—no disappointment, no bad attitude.

He took his role, coming off the bench, in stride, with equanimity and poise.

That is what impressed me about Jon Jaques.

He is selfless, to a fault.

However, as the season progressed, Mr. Jaques found himself installed as a starter. And, boy, did he thrive.

At 6'6", Mr. Jaques is imposing, but, as I have long since teased him, even at my advanced age, I sort of fancy myself in a footrace with him. Back in 2010, I'd have bet good money on my being quicker than Jon Jaques.

"Slower than molasses," I teased him then (and maybe a little now).

But could Jon Jaques shoot. He would shoot spot-up threes—just drain 'em. He'd find his spot, and then the ball would gracefully arc its way into the hoop.

His favorite spot was on either side of the key.

He'd steady himself and then, for just the tiniest fraction of a second, watch the ball as it left his hand, as if he wanted to bear witness to the fluid beauty of his shot.

And I, for one, would never blame him for taking the time to watch a Jon Jaques release. A couple of times over the last few seasons, I've caught the end of practice and watched him nail three after three.

All of a sudden, it's 2010 all over again.

I sell Mr. Jaques short. Yes, he could shoot lights out, but he could also use his shooting prowess to fake out an opponent. Jon Jaques could drive, and he could finish. And, he could, when the moment called for it, dunk.

However, I was not a Cornell basketball fan. I was a Jon Jaques fan. I still am.

This was not so with the 2023–24 Cornell team.

On the 2010 team, I knew Mr. Jaques, but only from a distance during the season.

With this team, I find myself deeply invested in them. Yes, I love watching them win. But I like them; I like staying after the end of a home game and talking with them, meeting their families. I've got some of their phone numbers. I text with Zeke, Chris, Manon, Nas, and Beccles. I know the dates of Zeke's, Manon's, Nas's, Adam's, AK's, and Beccles's birthdays. I know Zeke's little brother, Quincy's, birthday. (It's the same day as the greatest LFC player of all time, John Brian Charles Barnes, in case you're wondering. We'll meet him later. It's also Joni Mitchell's birthday.)

We've had some of the team over to dinner.

They drop by my class. We talk in the Ives hallways.

What happens to them is of consequence to me, to Ezra, and to Jane.

It's almost gotten to the point where it doesn't matter to me whether they win or lose. Although, of course, I want them to win.

I want them to do well.

I know that I'm keeping this journal in significant measure as a tribute to them. That's why I'll be bummed when Zeke, Manon, the Bricklayer, and Smooth Operator graduate. They'll leave a gaping hole in our lives—one, I have no doubt, Nas is more than ready to fill, and maybe Ragland, too.

An emblematic Nas story, as recounted by Zeke.

At the end of one of the team's practices, Nas says to me, "Mr. Farred, you should have us over for dinner again."

"Sure," I say.

I tell Zeke about this, and he comments, wryly, "Yeah, sounds like Nas. He's the only person who would invite himself over for dinner."

What's not to love about the kid from Nyack, New York?

I'm a fan. Of all of them. Look forward to getting to know Jake Fiegen.

One of the best aspects of being in too deep is that Mr. Jaques can take his place in my Cornell basketball affiliation—this time as associate head coach and, more importantly, as a member of a team.

And, later, as head coach.

That I singled him out the first time is of course not his fault.

But I think I like him better this way.

No matter what role he's taken—Cornell co-captain, deadly three-point marksman, Columbia University graduate assistant, husband, father, or associate head coach—his demeanor has remained unchanged. Jon Jaques is unflappable, intense, his eye always on the ball. Now he is cast in the role of teacher.

As his former teacher, I get to have the pleasure of watching Jon Jaques instruct players under the keen—and even more intense—eye of one Brian Earl.

8:17 p.m., February 19, 2024.

Standing on the landing as I'm writing in the living room, Jane announces: "Jake Fiegen is the Ivy League Rookie of the Week."
Fee-Freaking-. . O.

1:02 P.M., February 20, 2024.

My class, which starts at 11:40 A.M., is scheduled to end at 12:55 P.M.
Today, I go over time, finishing at 1:02 P.M.
As the students get ready to leave, in stride Nas and Manon.
"The MVP of the Ivy League," I say of Manon.
"Next season's Ivy League MVP" is the prediction I throw at Nas.
Manon, caught off guard, makes a hurried exit, and a brief one, after which he returns. Nas, on the other hand, embraces my prediction. Besides, he has business to handle with me. "You're seven minutes late," he says. This is at once a statement of fact and, coming from Nas, a mischievous accusation.
Nas tells me that he got my message inviting him, Ragland, and Beccles to breakfast on February 28, because it's Jiggles's birthday.
I suggest that we get Smooth Operator to come along.
Nas vacillates before smiling at the prospect of Ragland and Boothby at the same table for breakfast. "And," he says, "we should invite Fiegen."
"Yeah," he and Chris agree, "we should invite Fiegen because he is the Ivy League Rookie of the Week."
Guess it'll be me and this grab-bag five for breakfast.
Beccles's birthday is really just an excuse for me to sit down in Ragland's company. According to Zeke, Manon, Nas, and Beccles, Ragland is the epitome of unfiltered speech. I'm having breakfast with Id. And, in Smooth Operator's opinion, having not only played with Id for three years but also taken a class with him, Guy Ragland possesses a quite incisive mind, to no one's surprise, I'm sure.

Guy Ragland *(Courtesy of Cornell University Athletics)*

Guy Ragland: a man of many names. Id. Rain Man-ish.

This is bound to be fun. Even if it isn't, it'll be an anthropological gold mine: Nas, always with a quip at the ready; Beccles, prone to laughing at the least provocation (and, what is worse, Nas seems to have taken him under his wing; God help Beccles); Boothby, who, as the season and his time at Cornell draw to a close, appears ever more willing to hold forth; Fiegen, with whom I don't think I've ever exchanged a word. And all of us, I expect, will be held spellbound by the irrepressibility of Guy Evers Kennedy Ragland Jr.

C'mon, man, how's that not the coolest name ever?

I can't wait for that breakfast.

I'm taking the seat right next to Ragland.

9:15 A.M., February 27, 2024.

Turns out I don't have to clamor to sit next to Ragland.

By the time I arrive on my bike at 9:15 A.M., Guy is sitting on a bench outside the pastry shop.

It was his mother, he informs me, who insisted on him inheriting his father's name—names. They're historically significant, his second and third names, he explains.

"Evers" is for Medgar Evers, the slain Civil Rights activist.

"Kennedy" is for the United States' first Roman Catholic president.

His father was not keen on imposing these names on his younger son—Guy has three older sisters and an older brother. All of his siblings are much older than him, by decades, in some cases.

Clearly, Ragland's mother got her way.

"That's a lot to live up to," I offer. Ragland shrugs and smiles, his dreads flicking gently across his face. In that shrug and that smile are not only assent but, I sense, a deep understanding of what it means to be a young black man aware of what it is he has inherited. What has been bequeathed to Guy is no small thing. Inheritance through the name is rarely something borne without some measure of difficulty, as much a gift as a burden. Guy Evers Kennedy Ragland Jr. is aware of that which has been bestowed upon him. It does not appear to weigh him down. He knows what is expected of him.

For now, Guy seems up to the demands of the name—for now, the future of the Ragland family and its commitment to history, Civil Rights advocacy, the fidelity, unto death, of Medgar Evers to that cause, the youth and political promise of the Camelot president ("Ask not what your country. . ."[49]), complicated by the fact that it was that same president who led America into Vietnam.

Ragland and I talk before his teammates arrive, he with an easy intelligence and a familiarity with the world that impresses.

Breakfast turns out to be a lively affair, with Nas at the center of all the narrative action. Fiegen, for his part, is the most reticent but shows himself to be self-deprecating when teased, as Nas is only too happy to do. Beccles, too, is on the quiet side, as if the hierarchy of seniority is eminently mobile. This is what obtains in Newman, except on the court, where Fiegen especially but Beccles, too, have secured playing time ahead of some of the sophomores and the upper classmen. But in this social setting, it's talk in order of rank.

Nas and Beccles, I am happy to report, demonstrate a capacity for better dietary choices, and they all demonstrate a healthy appetite.

Brian Earl: Princetonian Gone Rogue?

Brian Earl, Princeton offensive devotee gone rogue?

When the class of 2024 entered Newman Arena for the first time in the pandemic fall of 2020, Zeke recounts, Brian Earl made an announcement. He was giving up the Princeton offense in favor of a fast-paced, full-court game. He was not giving up the Princeton offense in toto but in the main. From that season on, Cornell teams would press the opposition relentlessly, but especially when the opponents inbounded the ball. The effect of the back-court press, as far as I can tell, is twofold. First, it shortens the shot clock for the opposition, which can rattle teams that need more time to set up their offense. A team that struggles against the back-court press might also commit a violation—that is, it will not get the ball over the half-court line in the time allotted (ten seconds). Such a turnover will lead to more possessions for Cornell, a high-volume team. With Brian Earl's new up-tempo-style team, if there's a good shot early in the clock, the players are free to go ahead and shoot or to "run and gun," a label NBA fans were wont to use for Mike D'Antoni teams. Through all of this rapid-fire shooting, deliberate pressing, risk-taking basketball, Brian Earl remains stoic, almost unreadable. But I wonder how he reconciles his deep roots in the Princeton offense with this new style of play he has adopted; Earl also borrowed some of his fast-paced tactics from Klopp—once more, their paths collide.[50] Second, intense pressing is a high-risk, high-reward style of play. If the opposing team beats the press, they can almost count on their superior numbers in the front court, leading to easy buckets. From time to time, this is the outcome when Cornell presses high. The reward, however, is that apart from shortening the shot clock, if Cornell can force a steal, this leads to an easy bucket for them. Such a steal—and here Manon is past master—is the defensive equivalent of a dunk. It gets the team and the fans riled up. It gets Zeke clapping his hands furiously. It gets Hansen pumped up.

Still, playing at this pace, forsaking the deliberate buildup of the Princeton offense was a huge leap of faith by Brian Earl. In making this decision, he was ceding considerable control to his players. He was trusting them to execute. He was going against what I take to be a lifelong instinct.

He was breaking with the tradition he'd been schooled in, first with Carril and then, for three years, with Carmody.

Besides, Carril's and Carmody's teams were massively successful. In fact, in the 1997–98 season, Carmody's Tigers were ranked as high as seventh in the nation. That was Brian Earl's junior year. That team, like its predecessor, made it to the NCAA tournament, but unlike the 1996–97 squad, the 1997–98 team made it to the second round.

On his résumé, Brian Earl can boast that he made it to the second round of the NCAA tournament not once but twice. He went to the NCAA tournament three of his four seasons at Princeton. He was highly heralded and feared, especially by opponents who'd never seen so many passes, to whom the backdoor cut was an alien thing, to whom a deliberately paced game was an entirely unknown basketball creature.

In the fall of 2020, Brian Earl gave that up.

That is no small thing.

Sometimes, as I watch him on the sidelines during this season and see his fast-paced offense not sharing the ball or one of his more athletic players driving into the lane when a kickout would be the far more judicious and effective decision, I can almost see him wince. Internally. Brian Earl's face is, it would seem, semipermanently locked into a frown—the kind of frown that is almost indistinguishable from a scowl. In truth, I'm not even sure that it is either a frown or a scowl. Let's create a neologism, in honor of Brian Earl: the frowl.

On the sidelines, Brian is a study in the inscrutable. He's difficult to read.[51] You can only guess at the perturbations, at the churning. I wonder if he ever relaxes or manages an inside smile.

I'm doubtful. But I hope I'm wrong.

In truth, however, Brian has not completely given up the Princeton offense. Earl style still relies on rapid ball movement, on "sharing the rock," on coordinated team play, and, in moments, the backdoor cut will catch opponents by surprise. Fittingly, it seems to me, the sharpest exponents of the backdoor cut may be the Bricklayer and Zeke—guys who have demonstrably more patience and are most effective within a deliberate system, although Zeke has an occasional penchant for his own mode of freestyling.

And Zeke is good at it, too, as the final game of his Cornell career against the Ohio State University showed. Zeke flourished in that second half against Ohio State. But that's the exception.

But Hansen, I should add, is no slouch when it comes to three-point shooting. And Zeke can drive with intent to do harm. AK, too, has the appearance of a thoughtful, calculating player. But he has a three-point shot that has the promise of becoming increasingly lethal.

Somewhere in Brian Earl, the struggle between Carril-Carmody, on the one hand, and fast-paced, high-volume shooting basketball, on the other, is still not fully resolved. Or maybe I'm just kidding myself. The Carril-Carmody gene, deeply lodged as it may be in Brian Earl's basketball psyche, is fighting a losing battle.

Nas, Manon, Smooth Operator—these guys, with every passing game, are making the Carril-Carmody gene ever more recessive.

It must age Brian Earl, this inner conflict; surely it rages in him?

Or has it gone gently into that Carril-Carmody night?

Or does the ghost of Carril and the visage of the now-retired Carmody haunt Brian Earl at night?

Or maybe it invigorates him, just watching Manon or Nas streak down court.

Or maybe it invigorates him and gives him stomach ulcers, unsure as he is to the outcome of this streaking downcourt.

In fairness to Brian, Manon will sometimes do that to a person.

Maybe more often than not. Maybe with every freaking fast break that Chris leads.

It is fun for us up in the stands to watch, I must admit.

Gets our adrenaline going, that's for sure.

I can only imagine that it leaves Brian biting his nails because he never knows if this Manon drive is going to result in a resounding dunk or a deft layup; you never can tell if he's going miss the dunk or the layup and then foul an opponent because of his frustration.

Whatever it is Cornell's paying Brian Earl, it is not enough.

I've had Chris Manon in a class. The kid can charm all who come into his ambit. But he can also drive you nuts. You never know what you're going to get with Chris Manon. I would even suggest that Chris Manon does not know what Chris Manon is going to do. And then, just behind Manon, you've Nas coming up. Nas is as skillful as he is lippy.

Good luck.

Coaching this lot, it is only a matter of time before Brian Earl will no longer have to trouble his barber.

7:23 p.m., February 21, 2024.

Ezra's going to work out with Zeke.
   We get to the gym early.
   The gym is empty except for Adam and Smooth Operator.
   Adam, the premed Cornell basketball player, is holding a ball in one hand and a clipboard in the other. He's talking easily with Boothby, who's shooting from the free-throw line.
   Nip's warming up, doing stretches.
   I watch Smooth Operator take shot after shot with an easy motion, nothing more than is absolutely needed.
   I've given him the wrong nickname.
   I should just call him Crucible and then give him a copy of Arthur Miller's drama.
   A Boothby release is a basketball shot distilled to its essence.
   It is pure, fluid, stripped of all excess. No superfluity is allowed here.
   He shoots so effortlessly and with such unerring accuracy that I am surprised at the two or three shots he misses while I'm watching.
   If Boothby were a poet, he'd be a cross between Gerard Manley Hopkins and Gary Snyder.
   I say Snyder because of his confidence; Snyder's lines convey a quiet, unassuming assurance. That's how Boothby shoots—with such confidence that you only notice when he misses. I say Hopkins for the stripped-down beauty. On the rare occasion that he misses, you watch the next one, which

he makes, of course, and you're quickly reminded: this is what a basketball shot should look like.

We talk briefly after Boothby and Adam are done with the drill.

Adam remarks, "Orgo's not so difficult."

Indeed, "Dr. Tsang-Hinton," for you, maybe—but not so for the rest of us.

Winning the Ivies.

I'd like to see Cornell win the Ivies this year because it would break up the real Ivy monopoly.

For the last decade, the Ivy League has been dominated by the Big Three—Princeton, Harvard, and Yale—except for 2017–18, when Harvard and Penn shared the honors and Penn went on to win the Ivy tournament. Cornell's last triumph—before there was an Ivy postseason—came in Jon Jaques's senior year, 2009–10.

Since then, Mr. Jaques has played two seasons professionally in Israel, gotten an MA (Columbia), gotten married, and is the father of a daughter and son.

Last season's team featured the Buffalo, New York, native Greg Dolan. After Nas's season ended early with a knee injury, Dolan took it upon himself, consciously or not, to pick up the slack. Cornell finished last season with a disappointing 7–7 record, making it to the Ivy tournament as the #4 seed team, losing to Princeton.

This year's Cornell squad is composed of a squad that is far more balanced, and almost any of the regular rotation players can deliver on any given night.

AK's been a revelation in his sophomore year. Hansen, the grafter, puts in all the hard work. The Bricklayer grabs rebounds, defends stoutly, and is an organizing presence on the floor. He and Zeke appear to be the most effective leaders on the team. Ragland's cut down on his turnovers and added conviction to his inside game (in addition to his three-point shooting, which, when on, is deadly). Zeke was playing well until his injury, doing all the little things—a key steal, a strong layup, determined defending. No longer a starter, Boothby fits into the rotation nicely, making his threes, as the flow of the game permits, defending better, moving more confidently without the ball.

With every game, Nas seems to get stronger, his lateral mobility improving. Nas, like Chris, can make his own shots. And Nas brings a cheeky confidence to the game. Mouthy is Nas; he's not afraid to let the opposing bench know his high opinion of them, in the Queen's English, no less. Just ask the Brown bench what it is like when Nas drains a clutch three.

Better still, ask Brian Earl.

Ask Nas, and he'll break into that smile and just say, in a long, stretched-out syllable, *Noooo-Oh* . . .

Cooper's stroke is on the mend, and with Fiegen beginning to leave his mark on the team, this is a deep Cornell squad.

February 20, 2024.

As I am writing, my phone rings.

It's Jacob Beccles. He's just finished a stats prelim (midterm exam).

We've been playing phone tag. We make plans to meet for breakfast on the twenty-seventh, the day before his birthday, because they'll be busy on the day of.

We talk about Chris: "I've telling him this whole season that he's the MVP," Jiggles says.

We're on the same page, Mr. Beccles and I.

Chris Manon.

It's Chris Manon who makes the 2023–24 Cornell team tick. Chris averages two steals a game.

He plays lockdown defense. Chris can score, as Beccles puts it in our phone conversation, "at all three levels." Chris can drive to the basket, he can pull up and hit a midrange jumper, and his three-point shooting is like a dagger in the heart of the opposition.

There are some nights when it feels as though the opposition is at a loss as to how to defend him.

Last year, Chris showed glimpses of sheer brilliance, though such efforts were sometimes undone by bad decision-making.

This year everything seems to have clicked.

Yes, he is still prone to foul trouble. Yes, there is certainly the odd bad turnover.

All in all, however, he's a force to be reckoned with; he's the best player on what I hope will turn out to be the best team in the Ivies.

Of course, I'm channeling Zeke here—Zeke, who is spot on when he reminds me, again, that the Ivies are old-fashioned. The best player on the best team gets MVP.

This season, Chris is the standout player in the Ivies.

Back of my head the name "Bez Mbeng" rings, as if to put the brake on my partisanship.

Chris leads with his play. Hansen, Zeke, and the irrepressible Nas, among others, seem to have the verbal leadership angle covered. But Chris's perfor-

Chris Manon *(Courtesy of Cornell University Athletics)*

mance, game after game, speaks volumes. His athleticism is a thing to behold. Watching Chris dunk, I'm struck by how effortless he makes it seem. Chris can dunk with authority and then turn and get back on defense with the goofiest smile, as if he'd just executed a regulation layup.

I want Cornell to win the Ivies this season because I am so deeply attached to these guys, starting with the seniors. It would be nice to shift the balance of Ivy men's basketball power north, to central upstate New York.

But if I am completely honest, I want just as badly to see Chris get his due. The young man from New Jersey is worthy of the award—and then some. I'm rooting for you, Mr. Manon.

Who's rah-rah now?

Wistfulness, Regret.

For Christmas '23, Bug—my nickname for my daughter, Andrea—asks me what I'd like.

My answer: "A Trent Alexander-Arnold LFC shirt. #66."

Never one to miss a moment to set me straight, Bug responds, "But you're not even a fan anymore."

Touché.

I don't even try to explain to her, but my "TAA," as I refer to Trent, shirt duly arrives.

Still, at the time of writing (July 2024), it has the tags on. I haven't found the right moment to wear it yet.

Had I explained to Bug why a TAA shirt was important to me, it would have been a long-winded story full of the history of my LFC fandom and the ways in which it is marked by a profound discomfiture around my love for Liverpool and race.

It would have involved a trinity of figures, with TAA as the LFC player who—forgive the inappropriate geometrical analogy—closed the circle. I've written about this in *Long Distance Love*, and at some length, so let me recap as briefly as possible.

When I became an LFC fan, the club already had a long and ugly history of not signing black footballers. LFC fans have a long and ugly history of disparaging black players on opposing teams. The LFC dressing room—locker room—was long a hive of unsavory racists. Word has it that those 1970s dressing rooms were dominated by the likes of Tommy Smith, native-born

Scouser; Smith played for Liverpool from 1962 to 1978. Widely known as the Hard Man of those LFC teams, Smith was an uncompromising player. In fact, Shankly once remarked: "Tommy Smith wasn't born. He was quarried." Smith captained LFC from 1971 through the 1972–73 season, after which he lost the captaincy to Emlyn Hughes, arguably the worst racist in those LFC dressing rooms.

Into this environment stepped Howard Gayle, also a native-born Scouser. This was the team ethos that predominated when Gayle made his LFC debut in 1977, the first black player to represent Liverpool.[52] And he was a local lad, at that, one badly shafted by those who should have known better. Gayle's experience at LFC was bitter, to say the least.

If Gayle was LFC's first black player, John Barnes was the club's first black star. He is, to my mind, the greatest LFC player of all time, an honor typically reserved for the former LFC player Kenny Dalglish, the manager who signed Barnesy. I rank Barnes highest because he succeeded, brilliantly, in the cauldron of English football that was still rife with blatant racism: abuse from the stands, little protection from referees, and outright nastiness from opponents. But that Barnes-led Liverpool of the mid- to late 1980s played exquisite football.

The articulate, diasporized son of the Trinidadian (father) and Jamaican (mother) middle-class, Barnes was far better able to deal with obstacles that confronted him.

He excelled as an LFC player. More than that, by the end of his time at the club, he had made himself a beloved son of the entire city—Liverpool fans, their city rivals, Everton, and fans of the lower league club Tranmere Rovers; run-of-the-mill folk and the city's elite all came to adore John Barnes.

I had always imagined that with Barnes, the issue of LFC racism was, if not resolved, then quietly put to bed for me.

Premature, on my part. Premature.

After all, his had been a magisterial tenure at LFC. But, wouldn't you know it, racism will insist on its right to an afterlife.

In the history of this afterlife, there were a few moments that gave me cause for pause. One moment, however, has remained with me.

12:45 P.M., June 1, 2019: Madrid, Spain.

Later in the evening of June 1, 2019, Liverpool will beat Tottenham Hotspur (Spurs), another English Premier League club, 2–0, to win our sixth Champions League title.

After the game, Klopp will sing: "Let's talk about six, baby / Let's talk about six."

That's how you channel Salt-N-Peppa in Spain, more than thirty years after "Let's Talk About Sex" debuted (1990, on the album *Blacks' Magic*).

Earlier in the day, however, I was jolted out of myself.

I'd been invited to give a talk on football and race for the European Union of Football Associations (EUFA) during a symposium, organized around a lunch by my friend Patrick Gasser.

Before presenting my talk, however, I looked across the table from me, and there he was: Garth Crooks, longtime Spurs striker.

I'd followed Crooks's career, in part because he had started his career at Stoke City, which, from my early youth, had been my second team in England.

I introduced myself to Mr. Crooks. I recalled for him, a little breathlessly, how excited I'd been when Stoke City had signed him. Crooks was a local Staffordshire lad (the area where Stoke City is based; the full name of the town is Stoke-on-Trent, close to Shakespeare's birthplace, Stratford-upon-Avon). More historically, he was Stoke City's second black player but the first one since Roy Brown in the mid- to late 1940s.[53]

Crooksie signing for Stoke had been a big deal for me, growing up disenfranchised in apartheid South Africa.

Garth Crooks would move to Spurs in the summer of 1980. Like Barnes, Crooks is of Jamaican descent.[54]

Crooksie and I got talking. This is when he drew me up short and told me about the racism he'd faced as a black Spurs player at Anfield.

But Crooksie got his revenge.

In the Liverpool–Spurs Boxing Day (December 26) fixture in 1981, Crooksie scored a late goal to beat LFC, 2–1, at Anfield.

That shut the Scousers up, Crooks more or less said.

But what kind of revenge was it, exactly? Shutting up the Anfield racists on Boxing Day?

What kind of taste does that leave in your mouth? And what thoughts coursed through your head as you recalled that memory? In all probability, I owe Garth Crooks, of Stoke City, Tottenham Hotspur, and England an apology for what I might have triggered.

That is not the kind of thought you can put out of your mind—your club's fans shouting racist invective to a black man you're sitting next to at lunch.

In truth, however, the situation was infinitely more complicated than just Scouser racism. It was more of an indictment of all of English football. I found this out when I asked Crooksie about how the Stoke City fans treated him; his answer was revealing. "They protected me," he said. "I was one of their own."

What I did not ask, and in retrospect should have, was: How did they treat opposing black players? Say, Viv Anderson (Nottingham Forest, Arsenal, Manchester United) or any one of the three West Bromwich Albion (WBA) lads, Laurie Cunningham, Cyrille Regis, and Brendon Batson, who formed the goalscoring core of that WBA team? Three players collectively known as the Three Degrees, a nod to the 1960s female vocal trio from Philadelphia.

In other words, what is the value of localized prophylaxis against racism?

I suspect that for Crooksie, it was a matter of knowing that it was only at Stoke City's home, the Victoria Ground, that he could enjoy immunity from racism. At the Victoria Ground, Crooksie was surrounded by those committed to protecting their own. At those other twenty-one stadiums, Anfield no less than all the others, he was at the mercy of the opposition's fans.

Yet do I marvel at this curious thing, the logic that is local anti-racism, if that is the correct term. Which I doubt. That is, (the Staffordshire brand of) racism that protects the local black player but has no qualms about giving full voice to its worst impulses in relation to the other team's black player/s.

About two years after Garth Crooks had moved to Spurs, Stoke City signed another local black player, the winger Mark Chamberlain,[55] from Port Vale FC, a club situated about four miles from Stoke-on-Trent. Chamberlain's son, Alex Oxlade-Chamberlain,[56] would play for Klopp's Liverpool (2017–23).

Yet do I marvel . . .

I stayed at the Estadio Wanda Metropolitano long after the game was over. I watched the trophy ceremony, LFC players' faces beaming as then captain Jordan Henderson got his hands on the trophy LFC fans call Ol' Big Ears. I saw the LFC goalkeeper, Allison Ramsés Becker, sit quietly by himself in the center circle. I later found out Allison had been FaceTiming with his wife, who was about to give birth.

TAA.

I was just soaking it all in, being present to see my club triumph a sixth time over all of Europe.

From my vantage point in a rapidly emptying stadium, I saw something I'll never forget.

In the far corner of the Metropolitano, there he was, all twenty-plus years of him, playing keepie-uppie with his mates—juggling the ball and passing it, as though he had nary a care in the world. He'd just won the Champions League, but, still in his kit, here he was, just having a laugh with his best mates: Trent Alexander-Arnold.

Yet do I marvel.

He'd made his LFC senior debut just days after his eighteenth birthday.

He was born in West Derby, just a couple of miles from Melwood, which was then still LFC's training ground.

A local lad, our Trent is.

And he's black.

The unholy trinity is made up of Howard Gayle, native-born Scouser who was the victim of LFC racism; John Barnes, Jamaican-born, raised in London, who withstood racist invective (from the crowds, not from within Anfield) and became an LFC legend; and now Trent, who is black, grew up a Liverpool fan, and is the first native-born black Liverpudlian to captain the club.[57] (Barnes and Paul Ince, acquired from AC Milan, and current skipper, the Dutchman Virgil van Dijk, were the previous black captains.)

Trent stands third in my Liverpool hierarchy; first comes Barnes, then Steven George Gerrard (Trent's hero; another native-born Scouser and the most complete footballer, other than Franz Beckenbauer, I have ever seen), and then Trent.

My regret is that, having given up LFC, I won't be able to see Trent flourish. Klopp officially, I later learned, made him vice captain this preseason.

Virgil's getting on in years—he'll be thirty-three in July 2024—and Trent's primed to replace him.

Not being able to see Trent, game after game, lead LFC out onto the pitch, especially at Anfield—that will be rough.

Howard Gayle was of us. We treated him abysmally. Barnes came to us and made himself one of us. Trent is ours, through and through. He came through the ranks, this West Derby lad. He's been at LFC since he was six.

He is our very own, this black, native-born captain.

Sorry, Trent.

Yours is, in all likelihood, the last Liverpool jersey I'll acquire.

Thanks for playing keepie-uppie with your mates at the Wanda Metropolitano in the early hours of June 2, 2019.

The sting of what Howard Gayle endured will never lessen.

What you do with a ball—splaying passes, seeing angles that are invisible and unthinkable to ordinary mortals (that is, other professional footballers)—all while you are so calm, so utterly in command of yourself, has made you the very face of the club, my club, itself. I can only begin to tell you what that means to me.

My pride in you is beyond measure. My debt to you immeasurable.

I hope that you and Howard Gayle have had a chance to meet. I hope that you will, if only for me, make a serious effort to talk with Howard Gayle.

I'd appreciate it.

I miss seeing you, you, above all, Trent.

Call it nostalgia for the future. Or nostalgia that is already calling to me from the future.

That is my enduring regret.

A regret for what, I will not know.

A regret rooted in the past.

Loss, a loss for what I might have known.

Howard Gayle. John Barnes.

TAA...

February 23, 2024.

It's W. E. B. Du Bois's birthday today. In class yesterday, I discussed three of Du Bois's essays on why the Negro must demand to be educated. Du Bois acknowledged the importance of vocational—*industrial* is his word for it in his critique of Tuskegee's Booker T. Washington—training but recommended a classical education, of the kind he received as a student at Fisk University in Nashville, Tennessee, then at Harvard, and which he experienced in Berlin. Du Bois wanted this classical education to be available to all Negro students. We talked in my class about the role of the Talented Tenth, those Negroes to whom Du Bois assigned an onerous and historic responsibility: leading the race in its quest to acquire "culture" and "civilization." He envisioned an elite black class determined to receive an education in a nation largely antagonistic to such an acquisition; a black elite engaged in a struggle against a still-divided nation, one in which the wounds of the Civil War were still fresh; an educated black class already locked in political conflict with a defeated South, a South already planning the disenfranchisement of the Negro and determined to lay to waste the Thirteenth, Fourteenth, and Fifteenth Amendments to the U.S. Constitution.

With Du Bois in the forefront of my thinking this morning, I decide to write Jake Fiegen. I do so because I'm not sure that Nas, or Boothby, for that matter, will actually go to the trouble of inviting Fiegen. I send him an email.

The thing about all the players on Brian Earl's team is that they're unfailingly polite.

I receive two very prompt and polite responses from Jake Fiegen, the first at 10:57 A.M., the second at 11:15 A.M., both confirming that he will be joining us.

So far, there is no word on Ragland's availability.

Whether or not Mr. Ragland will deign to hang out with the likes of me is one thing.

Mr. Ragland withholding his presence, now that could be a deal-breaker.

10:28 a.m., February 23, 2024.

The prescience of the Cornell University Athletics Department.

The Cornell University Athletics Department sends out a campus-wide email informing the community of this weekend's athletic events.

In their promo for the men's basketball matchup against Yale, it's Zeke who features. With his trademark headband, he is shown issuing instructions to his teammates in no uncertain terms. Zeke is a study in athletic intensity and menace.

The Cornell Athletics Department must know something because, it turns out, this is going to be Zeke's night.

7:05 p.m., February 23, 2024.

"Tonight is going to be Zeke's night," I say to Nip.
"It won't be Chris who carries them tonight," I go on.
Call it a hunch.
"Tonight is the kind of game where players like Zeke and AK are going to thrive."

National Anthem.

Why is America the only country in the world where the national anthem is played before every athletic contest? It's played before every middle school, high school, college game I've attended, before every professional sporting event. What does playing the national anthem prove—American exceptionalism?

If the Premier League dared to play "God Save The King" at Anfield before a Liverpool game, there would be booing heard all the way from Merseyside down to the House of Lords in London.

Seriously, why this obsession?

All athletes, coaches, and spectators are asked to stand and face the flag, "to honor our nation," before the anthem begins to play.

If you didn't play "The Star-Spangled Banner" before the game began, what would happen? You'd become less patriotic?

Has no one paid any attention to the critiques of that great American philosopher of pragmatism, Ralph Waldo Emerson? Emerson recognized in America a nation that, as much as it was proudly postcolonial (in winning the War of Independence against Britain) and aggressively imperial (territorially and ideologically expansionist), remained haunted by a profound sense of insecurity. Is that why the United States insists that, at every opportunity, patriotism must be performed?[58]

Seriously, what will it take to overcome that history of insecurity?

The Newman faithful have the annoying habit, when the anthem's being played instrumentally, of punctuating the word *red*—as in "the rocket's *red* glare"—making their voices the instruments of *red*-ness.

On March 16, 2024, at Columbia's Levien Gym, the Cornellians around us make sure to enunciate that red when the anthem is played. The Cornellians take the liberty to be especially loud when the version of the anthem is instrumental. But they're no less emphatic when the anthem itself is being sung. They are consistent in their dedication to punctuating red, the Cornell fans. I'll give them that much.

Talk about projection and overidentification—as if that red belongs exclusively to them, wherever they happen to be.

Talk about proprietary.

It's our red, not yours. No brown, crimson, or green in the anthem, they'll have you know. But what about the "Red Scare"? Aren't Cornellians afraid of guilt by ideological association?

As someone not born in this country, I find it strange, this habit of yours, to say the least. I've often thought about just sitting for it, and sometimes I have. I did so once at a Cubs game, where Jane and I got looks fit to kill, and once at a Durham Bulls baseball game in North Carolina, where we got the same withering looks. I've decided to just stand and stare vacantly straight ahead—not facing the flag. But I stand, because sometimes you just have to pick your battles.

In the future, I might just make sure it coincides with my bathroom runs. *I'm no Colin Kaepernick.*

At my age, nature does have the fortunate habit of calling frequently. Problem solved—sort of.

It's more like *problem not so subtly avoided.*

It's more like, *I'd like to sit this one out, if you don't mind.*

It's more like I'm questioning my own political *cojones*—and coming up short.

Instead, I just take comfort in Wilfred Owen's war-weary caution against patriotism and the multitude of transgressions it seeks to hide: *Dulce et decorum est.*

Owen is that World War I poet who saw the best and brightest of his generation slaughtered on the battlefield. And, having seen that, he wanted no part of cheap patriotism.

How is it that a nation that so prides itself on rugged individualism is so conformist in performing its national oath? And why is it that this determinedly individualist nation takes such offense at those who do not—Colin Kaepernick—perform their patriotism? Is U.S. patriotism that mode of self-negating, philosophically speaking, rugged individuality that permits no contradiction and dissent? Why are those who will not engage in performative patriotism punished?

I should do better by Wilfred Owen and Ralph Waldo Emerson (with an honorable mention to Emerson's most able pragmatist heir, John Dewey).

Patriotism, the first refuge of scoundrels—that's the best I've got.

7:15 P.M., FEBRUARY 23, 2024.

Cornell starts the game at full throttle, as expected. Zeke gets the first six of the Big Red's first ten points. He drives hard along the baseline, getting to the hoop. Zeke's approach is the one that Cornell will have to adopt, because Yale is playing very good perimeter defense. Despite Cornell's jumping out to a first-half lead, Yale has pretty much taken away one of Cornell's chief weapons: the three-point shot. They keep tabs especially on Boothby, while the likes of Hansen, Ragland, Nas, and Fiegen are all kept under wraps.

In the first half, Yale seems low energy, as though they haven't quite shaken off the aftereffects of the Princeton loss.

At the other end of the floor, Yale's three-point shooters, especially Mahoney, aren't getting much joy from the Cornell defense, where everyone seems locked in, even though Yale's grabbing a few more offensive rebounds than I imagine Brian Earl likes.

Mahoney will finish the game with a team-high sixteen points. Matt Knowling scores fifteen, and the Yale point guard and orchestrator-in-chief, Bez Mbeng, notches twelve with four assists and three rebounds.

Does all the little things, and then some, Bez Mbeng. Orchestrates. Plays superb defense.

The Big Red go into the break with a ten-point lead, 37–27.

That's no small feat, holding Yale to twenty-seven points in a half.

The second stanza, it's a different ball game altogether.

Yale outscores Cornell from the off, and it's no surprise when either Yale gets close or, as they've threatened to do, takes the lead.

But Cornell fights back. With the game in the balance, and Cornell maintaining a slim lead, Zeke makes his only mistake in the contest. Grabbing a rebound and seeing a teammate streaking up the floor, Zeke attempts a long pass that ends up in Mbeng's hands. Cornell duly commits a foul, and Yale goes ahead.

Earl pulls Zeke soon after.

Almost as if chastened, when Zeke returns to the court, he is battle-focused—at least, that's my speculation.

Zeke plays lockdown D, knots the game at fifty-eight—this after Yale had taken a 58–54 lead that was then cut to a single point when Nas made a three-pointer.

Zeke makes one of two free throws to tie the game. Cornell scores again to go up by two points on a couple of Fiegen free throws, Yale matches with a bucket (60–60), and then it's ZT: Zeke Time.

Recognizing that Yale had taken away Cornell's three-point shooters, Zeke goes into drive mode—hard drive mode. Seeing lanes, creating lanes, Zeke has the Yale defense figured out. They can defend the perimeter, but as soon as you get into the lane, they're hack-happy.

Manon's off his offensive game tonight, scoring only eleven and not always making good decisions on defense, meaning that he spends much of the second half in foul trouble, eventually fouling out with 11.2 seconds left. But Chris does record three blocks and, per usual, chips in with his two steals. Nas is second top scorer with fourteen and also pulls down a team-high eight boards; Hansen and Ragland contribute six each.

Isaiah "Zeke" Gray

Around the four-minute mark, there is a nasty clash of knees between Nas and Yale's Mbeng. Nas comes off second best. I hold my breath. Last season, Nas's season ended early because of a knee injury. It took all of the summer of 2023 and well into November for him to even begin to get back to his old self. But Nas does come back after Chris commits his fourth personal. And he is in good enough shape to finish the game.

AK is solid, again, with nine points and four bounds, and Fiegen is playing such good defense that the freshman is in at the death. This is no small tribute to the lad.

But the final minute and forty seconds of the game belong to Zeke.

First, with a minute and nine seconds left, he drives to the hoop, makes the basketball, gets fouled in the process, and nails the free throw.

At the end of every workout with Nip, Zeke has him shoot free throws. Nip has to make three in a row before Zeke will call time on the workout.

Zeke knows.

Cornell takes a 63–60 lead, and even though Yale, with twelve second left, finds itself at the stripe for three free throws after Chris commits his fifth foul, it turns out that Yale's Achilles' heel is precisely that: poor free-throw shooting (eleven for twenty-six on the night, a lot of points to leave at the charity stripe). Mahoney makes one of three free throws, and Yale fouls Zeke, who duly obliges by making two of two, and it's game.

Zeke finishes the game with a team-high eighteen.

After battling that foot injury, which affected his mobility and maybe even messed with his head a little ("I was a little baby about it," he tells me the night before the game as he and Nip are done working out), this is a hell of a way to play your penultimate home game for Cornell. Zeke's entire family is in attendance—his mom and her twin sister, Zeke's twin sister, Zeke's little brother, and Zeke's stepdad and grandparents.

I couldn't be happier for the lad.

After the game, Zeke is beaming.

Earned, lad, earned.

Around the Yale bench, James Jones, I notice, is his usual dapper self. I like the look of his pocket handkerchief, a fashion accent I hadn't noticed when I watched him against Princeton.

Mr. Jones is easily, according to Nas, the best-dressed coach in the Ivies.

However, if Jones wins the *GQ* award, it's because there is no sartorial competition. It's all sweats with the likes of Earl, Henderson (Princeton), and Donaghe (UPenn).

At the end of the season, it's Brian Earl who takes home the men's Ivy League "Coach of the Year" honors.

But James Jones will have the final say.

February 25, 2024.

It's not a good weekend, it being Senior Night and all, to get a split.
Next weekend, when Cornell travels to Philadelphia and Princeton, would be, if not ideal, then OK.
A Split Senior Night weekend, it turns out to be.
Cornell's just never at the races with this one.
Graduating seniors Darius Erving, Evan Williams, and Max Watson start in place of Noard, Nas, and Zeke, and Brown jumps out to an early 7-0 lead.
But even when the regular rotation resumes, Cornell just doesn't have it.
Even so, Cornell only goes into the break down by just two, 43–41.
At the start of the second half, however, Brown really applies the pressure. The Rhode Islanders open up a double-digit lead.
Toward the end of the game, with about three minutes left, Cornell makes a run, closing the gap to three, 74–71, but they just can't get over the hump.
Walt Clyde Frazier, the greatest Knick of all and for decades now the Knicks color commentator, will always say that about teams trying to get back into the game after falling behind. It takes so much to make up the deficit that, once you've done that, you just don't have enough to take the lead.
What's worse, when they do have the chance to cut into Brown's lead, Nas (uncharacteristically), Ragland, and Hansen miss free throws.
Coming in at 1–7, Brown was there for the taking.
Cornell, Yale, and Princeton have already qualified for the Ivy tournament, but the Big Red, if it is to maximize its chances of winning the postseason tournament and booking its place in the NCAA tournament, some-

thing it hasn't done since Jon Jaques's senior year, needs to enter as Ivy League regular season champs, with the #1 seed.

Being seeded #2 or #3 will mean that they'll be playing either Yale or Princeton, not a matchup I'd fancy. In fact, with the Brown loss and Princeton having their final games at home, I'd pick the Tigers to finish atop the table.

In order to secure the #1 seed, Cornell would have to run the table. That is, they'd have to beat Penn (Friday, March 1), then Princeton the next night, before facing a Columbia team that looks to be running into form.

It's a tough ask.

I'm not optimistic.

That loss to Brown left me a little flat.

In order to learn how to win, you have to win.

Axiomatic, I know, but Princeton and Yale have shown that they know how to win in the Ivies. And last year, Princeton made a deep run in the NCAA tournament.

Brian Earl's squad will have to do it the hard way.

Last season, tough losses to Brown (on the road) and Princeton (at home) derailed their season.

They've done better this season, but 8-2 is not 9-1.

Again, the wise thing to do—as I'm sure Brian will be preaching this all week in practice—is for the team not to get ahead of itself.

Cornell needs to take first things first: all eyes should be on Penn.

Take care of business.

Handle your business.

Don't let this chance slip.

Win the Ivies, win the tournament, and this squad—with seven seniors—might be able to take the first step toward breaking the Big Three's Ivy monopoly.

You can't do anything now about the Brown loss.

You've got to learn from it, and learn quickly.

There are no easy games in this league.

Think of the color of an overripe banana.

Try to avoid slipping on the one that's coming up. Keep your teammates honest, Mr. Beccles, you Philly native, you.

Try not to slip up this coming Friday.

Like I said, this was a bad weekend to get a split. It means Cornell can't afford a split this coming weekend.

11:27 A.M., February 26, 2024.

"Walking around the campus," says Jane, who has just returned from her office, "made me think about your book."

She explains that, in writing *My Ithaca Journal*, I am simultaneously reversing the story of my Liverpool fandom and reinforcing it.

I wrote *Long Distance Love: A Passion for Football* (2007), an account, as the title makes clear, of how I became an LFC fan from afar. However, the distance was geopolitical—geographically removed, because I became an LFC fan as a disenfranchised boy growing up in apartheid South Africa, and, as such, inevitably political. But the distance never affected me as a fan. I poured my life into Liverpool, devouring—via print media, local Cape Town newspapers, British football magazines such as *Shoot*, British comics for boys, *Tiger*, *Scorcher*, and biographies and autobiographies of my favorite players, sports histories, and so on—all that I could, thereby negating the geographical distance without, of course, entirely overcoming it.

A Sports Odyssey, on the other hand, recounts a far more intimate set of experiences, including those involving our son but also the ways in which I have forged connections with the players and the coaches on the Cornell men's basketball team. It's my MO, Jane reminds me. It's always through the personal that I establish my relation to sports institutions. In the case of Liverpool, it would take decades for the personal to manifest itself—more than thirty years, in fact, because I only met John Barnes in March 2004. To be precise, I met John Barnes on March 18, 2004, having become an LFC fan in February 1970.

In the case of this Cornell team, it's Jon Jaques, Brian Earl, Zeke, Nas, Manon, Hansen, Ragland, Fiegen, and so on.

On March 18, 2004, I gave a talk on intellectuals at Liverpool John Moores University. What is more, I gave a talk with John Barnes in attendance, his presence secured by my friend Ross Dawson (not directly, but one of Ross's colleagues knew someone who knew Barnes). I shared drinks with John Barnes, lifelong teetotaler that I am, and I went to dinner with Barnes.

Tomorrow, I'm taking five members of the Cornell men's basketball team to breakfast.

As I've said, I am by no means an institutional animal. I am not a Cornell professor. I am a professor who teaches at Cornell. And I would insist upon that distinction. I taught at Duke University, but my entire intellectual life at that institution was centered around the Program in Literature at Duke University. For me, Duke University will always be not the institution as such but that unique cadre of thinkers—figures such as the late Fred Jameson, Michael Hardt, Ken Surin, VY Mudimbe, and Toril Moi, to say nothing of the various folks who moved in the Program in Literature orbit.[59]

It is for this reason that, whatever my critique of the five "other" Ivies, I would have to qualify it by saying that I am in no way overly enamored of the Big Three. My tenure in the Program in Literature gave me a closeup view of the remarkable minds just mentioned. Because I have seen these thinkers at work, the Big Three holds no appeal for me.

Through sport, I am, however, capable of making intense connections. The institution, of course, is not accidental to this process. The institution is, instead, I would clarify, the incidental facilitator.

Much as I can say that I liked some Duke basketball players, especially those I taught—and here I must make special mention of Luol Deng[60]—I had no time for the culture around that team or for its coach. Basketball is *the* sport on the Duke campus. Students camp out in tents in K-Ville, named after the iconic former coach Mike Krzyzewski, to secure tickets to Duke basketball games.

Duke students watch the game being played on "Coach K Court" in Cameron Arena. It is a truly unique experience to watch the fans, the Cameron Crazies, as they are known, at a Duke basketball game. The entire physical structure that is Cameron seems to rock and sway, literally, with the fans' energy. I'm glad I got to be part of it.

But Krzyzewski? I never warmed to him. He was always too much the Sunbelt Republican for me. On top of that, it was said that Krzyzewski only gave interviews, in terms of the national media, to the *Wall Street Journal*. He also supported Republican Libby Dole in her campaign for a North Carolina Senate seat. Mercifully, Dole lost.

Here, I must say, I run the risk of being reductive. For all his conservative predilections, Krzyzewski, to his credit, built a community center, dedicated in the name of his mother, Emily Krzyzewski, designed to serve Durham's ever-growing Latino population.

I attribute that to the Polish Catholic in Krzyzewski and admire him for having done such a thing.

After all, Polish Catholicism is a contradictory animal, in the contemporary moment, at least. On the one hand, Polish Catholicism has a very strong reactionary strain—think Pope John Paul II, Karol Józef Wojtyla, the pontiff dedicated to undoing every radical possibility contained in Vatican II. Vatican II was an attempt by the Roman Catholic Church to modernize in the early to mid-1960s. Among the major reforms Vatican II instituted were, perhaps most famously, allowing the Mass to be conducted in the vernacular rather than in Latin. Among the other changes Vatican II inaugurated was the incorporation into the structure of the Church the goals of the social movements then sweeping Latin America.

John Paul II did everything he could to undo that, making of the Church under his papacy a far more conservative and backward-looking institution. In my less sanguine moments, I attribute to John Paul's ideology (delayed political outgrowth) the rise and rule of Poland's Law and Justice Party. This party was overseen by the archconservative twins Lech (now deceased) and Jarosław Kaczyński, with their virulently anti-LGBTQ+ and xenophobic agenda. To my mind, Lech and Jarosław are John Paul's ideological grandsons, so true have been—were—these progeny to the Polish Pope's retrograde politics.

In addition to Law and Justice, there was the phenomenon known as the Mohair Brigade. This was a group of grandmothers, raised in postwar Communist Poland, who, with the fall of the Berlin Wall, dedicated their life savings to ensuring that their grandchildren all received a Catholic education. There would be no more Communist indoctrination, the likes of which had, to their minds, corrupted their own children.

Across the Atlantic, in a different conservative Catholic country, the women remained engaged in a different political project. Far from Warsaw, Wroclaw, and Cracow, in Buenos Aires, the Madres de la Plaza de Mayo, the mothers and the grandmothers (abuelas) of the disappeared—los desaparecidos—were still marching, as they had been since 1977, protesting the violence of Jorge Videla, the Guerra Sucia, and mourning the children and grandchildren they had lost.

On the other hand, who among us can forget the remarkable bravery of Lech Wałęsa's Solidarity Movement, which began in the shipyards of Gdansk and prefigured the end of Communist rule not only in Poland but in all of Eastern and Central Europe? It would take only a decade after Wałęsa, a shipyard electrician, organized the shipyards for the Berlin Wall to come tumbling down. Wałęsa, only modestly a man of faith, tapped into the radical ethos of Polish Catholicism, which has a history of standing against tyrannical rule.

Did Wałęsa, I wonder, draw inspiration for his movement from the brave women in Buenos Aires?

Might I propose Mike Krzyzewski as a moderate blend of the Mohair Brigade and Wałęsa—Mike Krzyzewski, that figure in whom Polish Catholicism, infused with Sunbelt Republicanism, presents its best, most publicly genteel face?

However one stands in relation to Coach K, it is nonetheless sacrilegious, even for a former Duke faculty member, to declare what I am about to: my (political) sympathies were always with the head coach of Duke's fiercest rival, the nearby University of North Carolina. (I like UNC, and I have rooted for them in NCAA tournaments gone by, but I'd never support them against Duke. It's complicated and contradictory, I know, but there you have it.) "The Dean," as the UNC legions call Coach Dean Smith, was born in Kansas but, as a man much disaffected by the white South, stood against 1960s segregation.

Smith attended the University of Kansas on an academic scholarship, majoring in mathematics. Krzyzewski graduated from West Point. Dean Smith, it is said, was fascinated by the philosophy of Søren Kierkegaard.

Dean Smith coached NBA stars such as James Worthy (LA Lakers), Sam Perkins (most notably the Lakers and the Seattle Supersonics), Rasheed Wallace (Detroit Pistons), Vince Carter (Toronto Raptors), and, of course, one Michael Jordan (Chicago Bulls). Today, one of Smith's African American graduates and a former Knicks guard, Hubert Davis, is the UNC Chapel Hill head coach.

When Krzyzewski, in many ways the face of the entire institution that is Duke University, stepped down two seasons ago, after having had a few former African American players—and very good ones, too (Johnny Dawkins comes immediately to mind, as does the current Harvard and former University of Michigan coach, Tommy Amaker)—on his coaching staff, his successor was a run-of-the-mill white (college) player, Jon Scheyer. Sorry, Johnny Dawkins (who starred for the Philadelphia 76ers), this door is closed. Don't even think of applying, Tommy Amaker. I'd also like to know what former white Duke players and assistants such as Bobby Hurley (University at Buffalo, currently head coach at Arizona State), who struck out on his own, make of Scheyer's elevation.

Though I am no longer at Duke, I can still root for Duke players (Paolo Banchero, for one; Ezra has an RJ Barrett jersey, although of the Knicks variety, not the Duke one), but I can never get behind Scheyer. He bears for me too much of the Coach K imprint, even from afar. Krzyzewski was, as he remains for me, a complicated figure, a figure whose complexity I lived during my tenure at Duke. Scheyer just leaves me cold.

I am allergic to Scheyer because I will always wonder why he got the job. Did Scheyer show himself to be that much better an assistant coach than Dawkins or Hurley, for that matter? All that is left for me is to admire Duke players. And with that, I have no problem.

One of the great things about Cornell men's basketball, then, is that I like Brian Earl, Jon Jaques, and their players.

I like how they are with their players. I like how it is Brian Earl sees the world.

I admire his capacity for self-reflection. His players, from my interactions with them, bear this out.

When Brian Earl met with his Cornell players, for the last time, to tell them that he was leaving for William & Mary, his address was brief. He was, his players recall, overcome with emotion, on the verge of tears. He left each of his players a note in their locker.

No small thing, that.

At the very least, it makes me feel Cornell losses keenly. It's not for me, losing. But I'm hardened against the sharper edges of defeat by my New York Mets (baseball), New York Lilliputians (Giants, gridiron), and, of course, New York Knicks fandom. Those teams will teach you all you need to know about losing in ways more painful than I care to explain. And I've got the psychological scars to prove it.

I want Brian Earl and his team to do well. That's how the local gets you. That's how the local gets to you.

But I am also honest enough to know that it will never sting as much as a Liverpool loss did.

Am I really being completely honest? Yes, as far as I can tell.

The long distance will always have that over the local.

Will it, really?

It is a higher order of pain, my LFC long-distance fandom.

Is it, really?

It is a pain that never goes away.

Trent: a pain that comes from who knows how many seasons hence.

But then again, never say never. Who can say what the local holds in store for you as a fan?

1:40 p.m., March 16, 2024.

I walk up Amsterdam Avenue to Columbia University's Levien Gym. The crowd going in the opposite direction is a mix of shocked and (happily) bewildered Brown fans—how did they win? That seems to be the look on their unbelieving faces—and on those of an array of equally shocked and (very unhappily) bewildered Princeton fans—how did they lose? *Lose, to Brown? Really?*

But what really catches my eye and hurtles me back to 1992 is the getup of the defeated Princeton fans.

It's like it's the Princeton Reunion all over again, displaced to Manhattan and restricted to the school's basketball faithful. I see blazers in all manner of orange and black, straw boaters, even on a biting March day.

One outfit, however, takes the cake.

The worst are full of bad fashion sense.

I see a late-middle-aged Princeton alum in a black Princeton T-shirt, black leggings, and orange fleece Hawaii shorts—the shorts dotted, as they should be, with black tigers.

The *cojones* on that guy.

Dude, you're just about in Harlem dressed like that?

You are laying yourself open to a citizen's arrest. The grounds? Offense to the neighborhood's aesthetic sensibilities. Who dressed you this morning? Who allowed you to leave the house looking like that? You walked around the whole day looking like that?

Get thee to a tailor, but quick.

2:00 p.m., March 16, 2024.

It is Cornell against Yale in the semifinals of Ivy Madness at Columbia University's gym on 120th Street, between Broadway and Amsterdam.

Yale jumps out to a 9–2 lead, and that's the closest Cornell will get for the rest of the game.

Actually, there is a moment in the second half when Cornell closes the gap: 50–57.

Nas is at the free-throw line for a one-and-one, but he misses the first, and it's pretty much game over after that.

It is a dispiriting end to what had seemed a promising season.

Jane and Ezra head back to our hotel in Harlem. I wait outside the gym, just so I can offer some small solace to the players and the coaches.

Or maybe in the hope that pain shared is pain diminished. Even if only ever so slightly.

I know it won't do any good, but it's my way of thanking them for the season.

The best I can hope for is that maybe I can absorb, momentarily, a little of their hurt.

I doubt it, but . . . it's all I've got to offer.

It's Elton John Time.

Elton John asks us, "What do I say when it's all over?" Then he proceeds to lament his "sad, sad situation" before not quite answering his own question: "Sorry seems to be the hardest word." I rediscovered his conundrum myself.[61]

Ragland is the first to emerge from the locker room. He stares straight ahead, still clad in his gear, intent on making his way to the bus that will take the team back to Ithaca. It'll be a long drive—a very long one. Fiegen's next, and he looks like he's done his due diligence; he's showered and has changed from his basketball gear into his gray Cornell sweats. Jon Jaques, the former Columbia assistant coach, comes through the door and, like Ragland, really wants the safety of the bus.

But not so fast. First, there are people who want to offer their sympathies, and there are others who want to thank him for the season. Mr. Jaques gets caught in a scrum of people, and I watch him dutifully engage. Even watching him from a distance, I can see he exudes disappointment.

Evan Williams is among those who follow Fiegen and Mr. Jaques. Evan, who didn't play, bears the demeanor of a man resigned. His Cornell career is over. He talks easily with a couple folks close to me. AK puts on his best face. There is an unmistakable honesty about AK: he does not dissemble. He gives the appearance of a thoughtful young man, one who knows that this was an opportunity missed.

Somehow, in the midst of all this Yale exuberance and Cornell disappointment, AK seems to find a spot, the smallest patch outside the gym, where he is able to stand alone.

And so they trickle out.

Now and then, a Yale assistant coach or player emerges, beaming, to cheers. Everyone is very happy to see them. To add insult to injury, as the Cornell folks wait, the Yale marching band strikes up a tune—understandable, though it does have a certain cruel edge.

But that is the fate of the losing team. You have to suck it up.

Family and friends wait outside for the Cornell players.

Chris comes out and, as is always true for him, his dad and his siblings are there. Chris, that famous Manon smile in effect, defeat or no, responds to his family with love and affection. If he's hurting, he's doing a good job of keeping it inside.

What's more impressive is that, as everyone will later learn, Chris sustained an injury to his left foot that will keep him out of the National Invitational Tournament (NIT) game against Ohio State.

Through it all, the Manon smile does the work of accepting good wishes, bearing up, and even dispensing good will. He is phlegmatic, our Mr. Manon; to the very end, Chris is remarkably immutably Chris.

He did not play well, but this "sad, sad situation" must be handled—and handle it, he does, with grace and characteristic charm.

Roger Kahn: You fall in love with a team in defeat.

If Chris is Kiplingesque, with a "treat these impostors just the same" attitude, Zeke's mom, with whom I share a hug, is distraught. She makes no effort to hide her hurt. I feel for her. There's nothing I or anyone can say to lessen the sting.

Like Chris, Nas shows poise and equanimity in defeat. His smile, unlike Chris's, betrays traces of disappointment. But he, too, takes the loss in stride as best he can.

He, too, did not play well, but at least he has one more year to put things right.

With Nas, of course, the question is always whether he will absorb the lessons learned in defeat and put it to good effect. With Nas, that is always an open question.

For his sake, I hope he can learn from this loss and then lead this squad through good decision-making come next season.

Only once does Nas let the hurt slip: "It's going to be a long year," he admits, acknowledging that the offseason, which could already have begun, will leave a lot of time to live with this defeat.

I talk with Hansen's mom, who evinces a singular pride in her son. She seems to me grounded, able to recognize the pain of defeat while also seeing the season—and indeed the Bricklayer's entire Cornell career—in its totality. Hansen, I would wager, has inherited his mother's capacity for equanimity, regardless of the outcome.

I tell her of my admiration for him. She tells me that he mentioned the book I gave him. I recall how wonderfully engaged he was at our house when he, Chris, and Zeke came for dinner. She is both pleased and unsurprised by her son's conduct.

"I want his jersey," I joke with her. She promises to pass my impossible request along.

At about this time, Zeke comes through the door, and there is no mistaking it: he is hurting. Like Chris, he is embraced by his family, his mom foremost. It is as if she is trying to absorb some of her son's hurt. She knows she can't, but it is almost too much for her. This could be the end of Zeke's Cornell basketball career, and this is not how either would have scripted it.

Zeke is putting on his bravest face. He looks shattered.

"I'm sorry," I say, as we hug.

I remark on how difficult this is, on how visible—and visceral, and raw—it is on his face. "I'm just trying to hold it together," he admits.

Still, Zeke—even in this, this most painful moment of his athletic career, I would bet—finds within himself the wherewithal to thank us.

"I appreciate you guys coming," he manages.

And that makes me hurt all the more for him.

I know that I said my Liverpool pain operates in a register and at its own level of intensity, but, in this moment, here on 120th Street between Broadway and Amsterdam, this feels awfully familiar.

But it also feels different.

It is different because the loss is not mine, different because I am helpless in the face of Zeke's loss, of Brian Earl's loss.

There is absolutely nothing I can do.

I can just stand outside a gym, offering what must seem to the principals like platitudes.

Brian is the last person I would offer platitudes to. He's much too straight a guy for that.

He is surrounded by people but, even as all this is swirling around, he asks, to no one in particular, as far as I can tell, "Where's Chris?"

In that moment on Saturday after the loss, that inquiry by the coach trying to find his player makes no sense to me. On Tuesday evening at 7:00 P.M., when the ESPN cameras cut to Chris in a protective boot, the reason for that inquiry reveals itself.

More important than that, however, is what it reveals about Brian Earl, the Cornell men's basketball coach.

His concern, as devastating as this loss must be, especially after a season in which his team showed itself to be one of the three best teams in the Ivies, is for his player.

He wants to make sure that Chris is OK, or as OK as Chris could be after the loss and sustaining an injury.

I turn and walk down 120th Street. It was on this street, in August 1989, that I lived when I first arrived in the United States.

I lived at 434 West 120th, apartment 4H—the Poinciana.

I felt, just for a moment, as if I were walking directly back into the past.

But in truth, I was walking away as quickly as I could, because I so desperately wished that the result had been otherwise.

I was walking away not from that long-ago past but from the immediate past.

I walked down Broadway, toward 125th Street, toward Harlem.

I had lingered long enough at the scene of defeat.

Brian Earl's Face.

As the team walks toward the exit after the final whistle, I catch sight of Brian Earl's face as he leaves the court. It has the look of both comprehension and resignation but not disappointment. Brian Earl *knows* why his team lost. Jake Fiegen apart, there is no one on the Cornell team who played well.

They did not share the ball enough. They did not make the extra pass. There were too few unselfish plays and too many poor decisions. There was not enough leadership on the floor. The players who should have demonstrated leadership did not. There was too much *me* and not enough *we*. There was too much SG in evidence.

Each in their own way is culpable: Zeke, Chris, Sean, Nas.

This is not how they wanted this weekend to go. This is not how they wanted their Cornell careers to end—with a whimper, a sad whimper.

For Zeke, Chris, Sean, and Keller, this is the end of the road as Cornell players.

Because of COVID, they will have the chance of one more year of college eligibility. But they'll have to take the lessons of this defeat with them wherever they play next—if they secure such an opportunity.

For Nas, it'll all be a lot closer to home.

If he wants to lead this team next season, he'll have to step up and make smarter decisions. He'll have to do what the team needs him to do to win. Everyone knows he can score. His talent and ability are not in question. But is he willing to do what it takes to win? Is he willing to do so if it involves giving the ball up at crucial moments or biting his tongue so that he doesn't get on the wrong side of the officials or if it means that his stat sheet will not be what he would like? Ragland, too, will have to share this burden.

It remains for me an open question: Can Nas and Ragland do this? Are they willing to do this?

Can they see the truth in the clichés—sacrifice, diving for the loose ball, playing hard-nosed defense, giving up your body to take a charge, making good decisions? Sure, as the leader, you want the ball in your hands at key moments, but before that, can you commit to making the extra pass? Are you willing to do everything you can to help the team win?

For now, the jury's out.

In short, can the next edition of the Cornell men's basketball team take their cue from their coach and their associate head coach? Jon Jaques quietly rode the bench as a senior co-captain in 2009–10. When his chance came, he not only took it, he absolutely reveled in it. And he reveled in it in the most team-oriented way. Mr. Jaques's three-point shooting opened up scoring opportunities for his teammates. Creating those opportunities gave Mr. Jaques, I am sure, as much pleasure as actually hitting those threes (OK, maybe not *as much*, but Jon Jaques was first and above all a team man).

Brian Earl knows what it takes to win.

As a player at Princeton, he won. As an assistant coach at Princeton, he won.

He *knows* what his players do not.

Their career accomplishments will not match his.

I am sure that Princeton losing to Brown, a team with a record far inferior to Cornell's, would have sat poorly with him, not only because he'd have, I'm imagining, some sympathy for his old teammate Mitch Henderson, but because he'd now have a sharper sense of the opportunity that his players had.

And he'd know that they did not seize it with both hands.

Carpe diem. It hurts when you don't win and you know you should have.

The Ivy Madness title was there for the taking.

And they didn't even get the chance to play for it.

That is what Brian Earl understood as he headed for the exit.

That hurts—when you know what could have been.

That is what the look on his face said as he exited. Stage Left.

Brian Earl *knew*. It may be that when you have won, as he has, and when you know that your team snatched defeat from the jaws of victory, the pain of defeat stings more sharply.

The only story that his players can now tell each other and themselves will begin, inevitably, as it must, *If only.* . . . You must learn how to win. The conditional clause speaks only regret. They will know, as you do, Brian, that they had it in their grasp.

8:16 p.m., March 16, 2024.

"I'm going to miss watching this team," Jane remarks ruefully after we get back from dinner at Sylvia's, Harlem's most famous soul food restaurant.

In truth, the food was just OK, although Jane loved the candied yams, and I thoroughly enjoyed the banana dessert.

Nip declares Shake Shack's burgers superior to Sylvia's.

Suddenly everyone's a food critic, even the out-of-towners from the provinces—as if Ithaca were a foodie heaven of some sort, as if we frequented high-end restaurants on a regular basis.

We don't. We're Blue Apron kinda folks.

10:56 A.M., St. Patrick's Day.

An email from Jake Fiegen informs me that Cornell will have another game after all.

The game will be against Ohio State University in the NIT.

This is a first for Cornell. It is a feather in Brian Earl and his coaching staff's cap.

March 18, 2024.

The Knicks play the Golden State Warriors in San Francisco.
　Josh Hart returns an insane stat line: 48–11–11–10, a triple double of some note.
　Hart plays all forty-eight minutes, he grabs eleven rebounds, he dishes our eleven assists, and he scores ten points.
　If there's any player on the Knicks I'd like Nip to emulate, it'd be Hart.
　Brunson's the star, but Hart's the heart and soul of this team.
　He makes an unselfish, all-out effort, night after night.
　With Randle still out, I marvel at how the Knicks share the ball. It is moved quickly, from one player to another, passed until it gets to the player best situated to take the shot. Miles "Deuce" McBride, promoted to the starting lineup, is *en fuego*, hitting threes with alacrity and, dare I say it, ease, as though he has suddenly morphed into Steph Curry. "Deuce" hits open threes, "Deuce" hits threes with defenders in his face. To top it all, "Deuce" guards Curry tough.
　"Deuce" scores twenty-nine points.
　I'm hoping it's a season-ending injury for Randle.
　But for the moment, I'm able to forget Randle and revel in Anthony Edwards's posterizing dunk. Edwards, star man on the Minnesota Timberwolves, absolutely owns John Collins of the Utah Jazz.
　Edwards's dunk demolishes Collins, who is cowering beneath Edwards, on the floor, literally, as the T-Wolves man slams the ball through the hoop.

Players on both the T-Wolves and the Jazz can do nothing but look on in utter disbelief.

A talented but high-maintenance player, Collins forced his way out of the Atlanta Hawks.

I bet he wished he'd stayed in Georgia now.

Ivy Title Game.

What can Brown do for you?

They can come close but they can't quite get over the finish line.

Brown dominates for most of the title game.

But, with less than three seconds left, and down by one, a bounce pass about three or four feet from the hoop by you-know-who to the senior Matt Knowling destroys Brown's dreams.

Yale: 62. Brown: 61.

Heartbreak for the Brown Bears.

We were rooting for Brown on the drive back to Ithaca, Jane driving, Nip next to her, me giving regular updates from the back seat.

Whoops of joy fill the car when Brown scores or defends, when Yale commits a turnover or Brown comes up with a good defensive play.

Two players catch my eye in the title game: Mbeng and his counterpart on Brown, the guard Kino Lilly Jr.

Sure, the Brown big guys Nana Owusu-Anane and Kalu Anya (both 6'8") play well, but it's Lilly who directs traffic, makes the big shots, puts the team on his back.

He played big in the semifinal to defeat Princeton and almost pulls off the big upset here.

He is a joy to watch—a player who leads while keeping his teammates involved, sharing the ball, making good decision after good decision.

Since Cornell can't win, you root for Brown. But you root even harder for Lilly, standing at six feet but playing so much bigger.

Mbeng, for his part, really has no shot—certainly not one you fear, like Lilly's or Smooth Operator's.

But the entire Yale offense runs through him. He always seems to make the right pass. He always seems to find the open man. And not for nothing is he Ivy League defensive player of the year.

In that final, game-changing play, with less than three seconds left on the clock, Mbeng was in a position to take the shot. The center, Danny Wolff, could have taken the shot. But neither of them did. Mbeng did what he does so well. He kept his head, he made that pass to Knowling. Mbeng opted for the simple, defense-splitting bounce pass. Knowling, one should note, is not the best shooter on the Yale team. The Yale shooters are August Mahoney, deadly from beyond the arc, and John Poulakidas, only slightly less likely to punish you from three-point land. But Mbeng trusted Knowling. The senior did not let his on-floor general down. Kudos to Knowling. A tribute to the leader, Mbeng is.

To James Jones and his staff's credit, when Knowling's shot goes through the rim, the Yale players and coaching staff not only mobbed Knowling, they were all over Mbeng as well. That is the culture, as folks are apt to say, that Jones has, over some twenty-eight seasons, inculcated at Yale.

That is how you win.

You make the extra pass. You trust your *teammate*. That's how *we* beats *me*.

You have a team leader who does not have SG.

Who gives you hope that just for a moment SG is returned to its (LFC) truth. To its best iteration.

What can Brown do for you?

Try as they might, much as you want them to, they can't beat Yale for you.

What you get is the opportunity to watch two distinct, contrasting forms of point guard leadership.

And you can admire both Mbeng and Lilly.

You go into a game wanting one outcome, and you emerge from it, having seen what Mbeng and Lilly do, feeling just a little chastened and like you've learned something you didn't expect to learn.

That's what Brown has done for you.

March 20, 2024.

My friend and colleague Tim Campbell and I talk over the phone about our Knicks.

Though we're both naturally pessimistic, for once, we're able to just enjoy our team.

Tim and I, like Nip and Tim's sons, Ale and Nico, hate Randle.

Tim and I talk about how freely—by which we mean unselfishly—the ball moves with Randle out of the rotation.

We wax lyrical about Josh Hart.

And we speak longingly of a potential OG Anunoby return.

The thing about Anunoby, I tell Tim, is that there's no evidence that he has a beating heart.

OG is entirely without affect. Looking at Anunoby's face, whether he's on the court or on the bench, you would not be able to tell if his team is up by three or down by forty.

Tim responds, "Anunoby's a cyborg."

Tim's nailed it.

And here I thought I was being clever referring to OG as "Original Gangster."

Nope, Cyborg just works better.

Part man, part machine, he is the only basketball player who, other than Kawhi Leonard, can mesmerize you with his silence—a silence that is neither obdurate nor forced. It is the silence of a Zen meister.

He is a man totally in control of himself.

He's a man whose silence silences you—into admiration and into gratitude.

Tim and I both miss IQ, but, boy, do we marvel—in silence, of course—at having OG on our team.

Much as Tim and I love IQ, we know that he did not perform in the playoffs last season.

As for RJ Barrett, who did perform well in the playoffs, you just get the feeling that he's got a ceiling, and that ceiling doesn't go high enough to get you to even the Eastern Conference Finals in the NBA.

I'm not saying that the Knicks will get there—please do not misunderstand me—but I'm pretty sure we would stand much less of a chance with IQ and Barrett on the roster.

So, Tim and I are in agreement that the catastrophically hapless Knicks brass, who have a history of making terrible trades, of signing the wrong players to contract extensions (Carmelo Anthony, Randle, need I say), have actually made a good trade this time.

They gave up two basketball players and some draft picks for a cyborg.

I'm taking the cyborg. All we need now is for our cyborg to be more cyborgian; that is, OG has to stay healthy.

If that's OK, of course, with you, Mr. Anunoby.

It turns out, he can't do it.

He limps out of the playoffs.[62]

This leaves Brunson to carry the scoring load and Hart to do just about everything, including scoring.

But we all know how this movie is going to end.

The best lack all conviction.

The same way it always has.[63]

March 19, 2024.

Turns out that Cornell has one more game left—against Ohio State in the NIT.

Chris is out. Inserted into the starting lineup—for the last time—is Smooth Operator. If there's any hangover or disappointment from the Yale performance, it is not evident this evening.

The fast pace at which Cornell plays—Cornell's quick shooting (something like using only fifteen seconds of clock for each shot)—gives the Buckeyes fits.

Cornell jumps out to a 19–9 lead. Ohio State closes in the final four minutes and twenty-eight seconds with an 18–4 run to go into halftime with a 44–38 lead.

Cornell should have been closer. Beccles misses two open layups, and this will cost Cornell dearly at the end.

But this Cornell team performance is a far cry from their desultory game against Yale, where they appeared tight, where there was an absence of energy, not to mention joy.

They share the ball. Cooper Noard's hitting threes; Ragland appears rejuvenated; Hansen, despite the six stitches he took in the Yale game, is full of confidence; Nas handles the point with a restrained ease. And Fiegen plays like only he can, doing all the little things and making his shots, too.

But Cornell is outmatched in terms of size. At 6′8″, Hansen and Ragland are no match for the Ohio State bigs, and in the first five minutes, Ohio State has already tallied ten *offensive* rebounds.

But Cornell won't go away.

The second half is Zeke Time.

The "senior from Brooklyn," the commentators keep saying, just explodes. He drives to the basket, playing defense as though someone were threatening to relieve him of his baseball hat collection (Zeke has an impressive collection, it must be said), totally pumped.

It's the best I've ever seen Zeke play.

The clear leader on the court, he makes a career high nineteen points, going 8-10 from the floor, plus five assists and four rebounds.

Zeke is driving with authority.

Zeke is taking charge.

Jane, Nip, and I are so freaking happy for him.

Granted, he does miss a key layup. With the score 84-81 in favor of the Buckeyes, Zeke makes a lovely cut from the left elbow and, with an open basket, misses the layup with his right hand. Had he used his left hand, he'd have had a better chance.

As he walks off the court disconsolate, Zeke takes off his trademark headband (either red or white, depending on the Cornell colors in that particular game), and I see him mouth "F-ck."

He knows how close he was to making it a one-point game.

Cornell loses 83-88, but what an account they gave of themselves.

Yes, they'll know they should have won. Yes, had Beccles made even one of those layups, it would have been a different ball game. Who knows if Ohio State might have folded should Zeke have made that layup. What might have happened if Nas hadn't driven into traffic, only to commit the turnover that finally put the game to bed? (There's a pattern here, Mr. Williams. Let's break it.)

If wishes were horses, beggars would ride, my mother was wont to tell us as children.

They'll rue this loss, Brian Earl and his squad will.

But they'll also know that the game against Ohio State was as much about winning as it was about redemption.

It was about giving this group of players one last chance to show that they can, on any given day, match up with teams that play in conferences more highly ranked than theirs. (Much more highly ranked, it should be said. Ohio State plays in the Big Ten conference, one of the power conferences in the nation.)

Brian Earl's squad won twenty-two games in the 2023-24 season, the fourth most in the nation.

And they were so close to a historic twenty-three—a win over a team from the Big Ten conference.

At the very least, Zeke, Hansen, Boothby can now leave the Cornell University men's basketball program with a measure of pride restored.

The Ohio State loss doesn't sting for me.

The only feeling I'm left with is pride.

You Lose Something When They're Gone.

This feeling is followed by a sense of loss.

I won't see this group together again—ever.

I won't be able to cheer for them again—ever.

And for that, I am the poorer.

It makes more of a difference than I ever imagined it could.

If you get to know a group of players and their coaches and get close to them, you lose something when they're gone.

It is loss that permeates A Sports Odyssey. This is a writing that was motivated by loss. Jürgen Klopp announcing his impending departure from Liverpool. That was the first blow. Then my slowly coming to understand that Jane's, Nip's, and my time with Zeke, Manon, the Bricklayer, and Smooth Operator was drawing to a close. Blow number two. And then, the nail in the coffin, Brian Earl making public his decision to leave Cornell for William & Mary. That is a tough trifecta.

It is a lot to take in.

I am not sure that it is even possible to take it all in. Or that you should.

If Brian stays, there's at least one thread of continuity.

The conditional, as I've said, counts for little.

The Algerian-French philosopher Jacques Derrida says that there is a singular truth to political struggles: one must always know that one will have to begin again. As if for the first time.

Fair enough. But Derrida offers no prescription as to how one begins again. At some point, I'll figure it out. As fans, we always do, don't we?

But that moment has not yet arrived for me.
And this writing about them provides little in the way of solace and succor.
Sometimes, as in this instance, when you're not even aware of it, your geographical local inches its way into your psyche.
Before you know it, you've learned to love a team.
And now you'll have to learn to live without them.
There is no room for platitudes. It remains only to admit that losing this group of players does not feel good to me.
I know only this: you lose something when they're gone.

The New York Knicks.

This leaves Nip and me to root for the Knicks.

They play the reigning NBA champs, the Denver Nuggets, tonight—March 21, 2024—and I'm looking forward to the game.

Apparently, OG Anunoby will be back, not tonight, but shortly.

The word on Randle is that he's not yet ready for physical contact.

I ask only that the basketball gods throw me and every long-suffering Knicks fan a bone.

Keep Randle on the sidelines—until at least next season.

I feel like I'm owed this one.

Please.

For a few more games, Nip, Tim, and I would like to dream.

Without conviction.

We dream about a lineup that features Jalen Brunson, Josh Hart, Isaiah Hartenstein, and OG Anunoby. We dream of a team lead by a star in Bruson, an otherworldly presence in OG, the indefatigable sparkplug that is Hart and the ever-willing black German-American Hartenstein.

I know, I know; it is too much to ask.

But I want to see this Knicks team do well in the playoffs.

I'm not asking for a championship—I'm too terrified of offending the gods to make such an importune request—I'm just asking for an extended playoff run.

That would make it easier to endure the loss when it happens, as it inevitably does.

That way, I can at least say that for the 2023–24 basketball season, I rooted for two teams I liked.

In fact, these were two teams I really liked, even more than I care to admit. I'm talking *like* like, the way awkward adolescents express their interest in someone to whom they're attracted.

But I've no doubt you've already caught on to my prevarication, to my ducking and weaving around the question of falling in love with a team.

Maybe that's just a truth too obvious to admit to, at least for now. How could I do what I promised myself I was not going to do?

Here I find myself embracing, as I never have before, the lure of the local, and in embracing it, I give the local inflections I did not know I could. I situate myself in relation to a place, Ithaca, as I had no intention of doing.

And much as I would like to, I can't blame it all on either Brian Earl or Nip, who are each in their own way culpable for leading me into this place, into this local, in this deeply invested way. I just wish I could blame it on those two. And I'd have good reason to, if you ask me.

If I hadn't had that accidental encounter with Brian Earl, I'd be going along merrily, not a Cornell men's basketball worry in the world. If I didn't have a son who has a modest talent for the game, I wouldn't have met Zeke. Again, I'd be going along very nicely, thank you, minding my own business.

But, no, the fates conspired against me.

So, as you can see, I had no choice.

What makes everything worse is I'm just not up to the demanding antiheroic standards of my antihero hero, Greg Heffley.

If I did have Greg Heffley's epistolary talents, I'd make of Brian Earl a Rodrick and of Nip a Manny.

Unfortunately, Brian Earl's no Rodrick (Rodrick wouldn't so much as sniff Princeton, and he's much too low energy, too much of a Gen Z wastrel, to even pick up a basketball, let alone play the game), and even though Nip does have the capacity to annoy me in a Manny-like fashion, he's too old for that analogy to hold.

So where does that leave me?

Well, it leaves me with nothing but *My Ithaca Sports Journal*, with its unreliable chronology, its constantly shifting locations, and, worst of all, its random ruminations on subjects that have no apparent relation to what is being diarized, all of which makes of me a poor journalist and *My Ithaca Sports Journal* a poor imitation of Greg's *Diary*.

Those basement philosophers of the 1990s, Garth and Wayne, put it best, Greg: "I am not worthy."

Bob Dylan.

The answer, I'm told, is "blowin' in the wind."[64]

Autochthony—that's the answer, an affiliation that defines your very being.

It is what you are.

At my core, I am Liverpool Football Club.

I am LFC. It is in *me.*

I will always be LFC.

I can never expel it or expunge it from my being—nor would I ever want to.

It does not "complete me," as that famous line from *Jerry Maguire* goes. It *constitutes* me.

Ontology. That is the term that philosophers who submit to the logic of essence would invoke.

That's the difference.

I will always support Brian Earl.

I will always root for Zeke, and Manon, the Bricklayer, Nas, and Smooth Operator.

I will always want success for Jon Jaques.

I suffer when the Knicks lose, when the Mets collapse, when the Lilliputians blow a lead.

But it is a lower order of pain.

It is, if you will, a flesh wound. It heals, eventually, even if not always quickly.

With Liverpool, I bleed internally. My entire being is at risk.

Maybe autofascism, then, is the only prophylactic against this, the most intense pain—the kind of pain you can only know when your very soul is on the verge of destruction, when your very being seems about to explode into a million fragments. Conversely, autofascism denies the possibility of a euphoria, the explosion of joy, happiness, contentment, and exhaustion the likes of which those who do not give their very being to a football club will never know.

That stratospheric joy is reserved for those who, to pluralize the rock guitarist Joe Satriani, "surf with the aliens."

I reveled when the Giants won the three Super Bowls—XXV, against the Buffalo Bills, the "wide right" thriller; XLII, with David Tyree's "miracle helmet catch"; and XLVI, with Mario Manningham's "sideline catch."

I thrilled *inside* with every Liverpool triumph.

The Mets, Knicks, Giants, and New York Rangers (the National Hockey League team I support)—those victories are external. I can share them with other human beings.

My Liverpool losses and triumphs I commune only with myself. LFC losses and wins are retained in and restricted to my core.

They are not for sharing. They are not for public engagement.

They are deeply and intensely proprietary.

They are *mine. And mine alone.*

Who knows how much we can bear that which defines us?

How long can we endure that which is so resolutely within us?

These are not answers that drift on the Dylanesque wind.

These are forces that churn, relentlessly, unceasingly, within us.

What they do to us, these forces, we cannot share—in part because we do not want to but in equal measure because these answers, we know, are always beyond our grasp. They will not submit to comprehension.

And so we allow ourselves to emerge from the inexplicability of our ontology into the visible, rational world.

We emerge into the external world, where answers can be discerned and explanations make sense.

But in so doing, we hide the truth of that which is us.

We know that even if we could, we would not share that truth.

About that truth, we are more jealous and felicitous than lovers.

But what we have to give externally—please do not mistake its value.

It is sincere. And it is no small thing.

It belongs to a different order.

And so it is constructed out of its own truth.

It will give everything external that it has to give while withholding everything that is inside.

In this way, the end of fifty-two years of LFC fandom is that question for which there can be no answer.

That much, I have learned, is obvious—and not always painfully so.

But there are moments, even today, in which I hurt. I hurt about Heysel and Hillsborough. I suffer for losses decades old (Wimbledon, 1988; Arsenal, the Mickey Thomas goal, 1989) in ways more than half a century has not taught me to overcome or endure.

What does it say about me that the losses stay with me more than the triumphs? That the losses are buried more deeply in my psyche?

Liverpool Football Club will never leave me because I can never leave it.

My *Sports Odyssey* leaves me in Ithaca in a Dylanesque state of reflection: "How many roads must a man walk down / Before you call him a man?"[65]

After all of this, what kind of fan am I? What kind of fan's name are you to append to me?

As such, *A Sports Odyssey* must be reckoned a failure of Dylanesque proportions. So many roads—LFC, Cornell men's basketball, the Knicks primary among them—I have made you walk down, and I still cannot tell what you by what fan's name you should call me.

I confess because I, who should have an answer, do not have one.

At the very least, however, I hope that you can understand that it is because it does not belong to my ontology that I can, as I have tried to explain, continue to support the former coach, the current coach, and those players to whom I have grown close. And, to repeat, my support means no less even then. It simply belongs to a different order of fandom. The Knicks et al. belong to this other order.

Postscript: 9:37 a.m., March 24, 2024.

It began with a text. It ends with a text. Things have come full circle.

It began with a text from Brian Earl. It ends with a text about Brian Earl.

The text is from my friend Chris Kerber, currently the head rowing coach at Hobart College in Geneva, New York.[66]

As it turns out, Jane, Nip, and I are on our way to Hobart College. We're going to Hobart because Nip has a workout with the Hobart men's basketball coach, Stefan Thompson.

I receive two words from Chris: "Jersey Legend!"

Accompanying the text is a story with the headline: "Brian Earl Resigns as Head Men's Basketball Coach at Cornell."

"Brian Earl resigned," I tell Jane and Nip.

A painful silence follows.

The Postscript's Postscript: Subtext.

"The lady doth protest too much, methinks."[67]

Things have come full circle.

It was Brian who informed me of Klopp's resignation.

"He needs a vacation," was Brian's recommendation. To be fair, Klopp and Pep are the only two coaches who, as far as I am aware, have ever taken sabbaticals. Klopp's was shorter than Pep's, which lasted a year and which, as you know, he spent in New York City.

Klopp's lasted less than four months. He left Borussia Dortmund in June 2015 and took the LFC job in mid-October.

Next season, Brian will be the head coach at William & Mary in Williamsburg, Virginia.

Where he will be joined by Smooth Operator, who will be completing an MBA at William & Mary. Just watch Keller Boothby drain threes against the likes of the College of Charleston in the Coastal Athletic Conference.

Brian Earl told everyone, not once, but twice, that he'd run his race with Cornell.

The Bricklayer from New Jersey is going to pursue a master's degree in engineering at George Washington University. They'll be adding a standout player and model student to their roster in you, Mr. Hansen.

With Brian Earl, you have to trust what his face tells you.

Chris Manon is off to Nashville, Tennessee, where he'll be doing something vaguely related to the law at Vanderbilt.

"It's the SEC," I remark to Chris. "Tough conference."

"I know," Chris responds. "I want to go up against the best."
Be careful of what you wish for, Chris.
I'm keen to see how things go for you against Alabama and Auburn.
Buena suerte.
Granted, Brian Earl's is a difficult-to-discern face. It gives away little, and even his smile gives you just enough room for doubt.
Zeke, as Nip might intone, is taking his talents to the University of Akron.
Zeke's performance in the game against Ohio State did wonders for his stock.
He was even offered a spot at Duke. Most likely at the end of the bench, meaning he'd have seen very little playing time.
Zeke just wants to play.
Akron's getting a dog from Brooklyn.
Zeke has anointed Nas as his successor, so come the autumn, Nip's coaching will be under new management.
I almost dread to think about Nas and Nip in the gym together.
For his sixteenth birthday, Nip asks his sister, Bug, for a Dennis Rodman Chicago Bulls jersey.
You can see where this is heading.
Rebounding, that part . . . fine. Already Ezra has plans to dye his hair multiple colors. Can regular trips to Pyongyang be far behind?
Zeke assures me that it will be OK.
You see why I take Zeke's assurances with a grain of salt—because I know that it is not Zeke's fault; I know that Zeke and I are helpless in the face of Nip's Nassian/Rodmanian predilections.
Zeke says that he'll be keeping tabs on the two of them.
One, I am not sure how that's going to work; two, I am not sure that even Zeke can keep Nip and his new instructor on the straight and narrow.
Meanwhile, this summer, Nip is working out with Guy.
Jane and I like it because Guy just towers over Nip. Makes our son look tiny by comparison.
Zeke's are big shoes to fill.
Even allowing for his indiscernibility, the look on Brian Earl's face as he passed through the doors at Leven Gymnasium, heading for the Cornell locker room, was not, as one might first have imagined, one of resignation (pun intended) but of finality.[68]
It spoke volumes, articulately. He had done what he could at Cornell, building a program envied not only in the Ivy League but more widely in the world of college basketball. He had done what he could with the resources at his disposal. He built a competitive squad, showed remarkable basketball ingenuity, born out of flexibility—the willingness to go against the grain of his own training and instinct. Against the odds, he fashioned a style of play that, especially in terms of its relentless pace, had produced competitive

performances against the likes of more highly regarded opponents (Boston College and Miami, 2022; Syracuse, 2023). Granted, the game against Baylor in January 2024 was one-sided. But his final game, against Ohio State, showed just how difficult an opponent Cornell had become and how innovative and sought after, it turns out, Coach Brian Earl had become.

Second, however much his squad restored pride with that performance against Ohio State, the look on his face after that game was not that of a coach about to take the "moral victory" of that defeat as a building block for next season.

Brian Earl's face after that NIT loss bore a terminal look.

He was done.

Now, I am tempted to muse that when he texted me about Klopp's resignation, he was telegraphing me his own impending departure.

That was the subtext.

I might have sensed it. It was prescience that I lacked.

Or maybe it just shows how good a poker player Brian Earl is.

Even when you're watching him closely and think you've got a bead on him, you have no idea as to what his next move is going to be.

The athletic powers-that-be in Williamsburg have made a smart hire.

In the wake of the defeat to Yale in Ivy Madness, it seemed ever more likely but not inevitable.

In no way, however, was I prepared for it.

I wish Brian Earl, his wife, Jen, and their three sons, Dylan, Owen, and Cooper, the very best.

But in no way can I disguise my own deep sense of loss.

Is this how the local loses its luster?

I fear that it might.

But I will be rooting with all my might for Coach Jon Jaques.

This brings us to the neat conclusion of *A Sports Odyssey*: "It's a sad, sad situation."

And I am going to follow the results for George Washington, Vanderbilt, Akron, and William & Mary.

Plus watch Cornell games.

I've got a lot of keeping track to do.

To say nothing of the prospect of watching IHS in Nip's sophomore year.

A prospect that, even as I write in the summer of 2024, fills me with more than a little dread. (After another losing season as a sophomore, Nip too, a year after Brian, Zeke, and Chris have left, decides that he is done with basketball in Ithaca. He is, as he is prone to say, "taking his talents to Minnetonka High." Again, IHS can muster only two wins, none of them in conference play. Nip establishes himself as a starter, but the prospect of two more seasons . . . that he will not bear.)

A writing that began in a keenly felt loss ends in a loss, one perhaps more deeply felt.

It is how this final loss cuts so close to the bone that surprises.

Perhaps, in truth, I should not have been surprised.

I was setting myself up for this all along.

But I didn't know it. I didn't know because I didn't think it possible.

How wrong I was—how wrong.

One way or another, my relationship to the Cornell University men's basketball team is going to be different.

How? That I cannot say. That difference, and the way in which it will manifest itself, I do not, at this moment, want to contemplate.

For the moment, I want only to tarry with this loss, to wonder if I shall, once again, take my distance from the local.

To know that I might take my distance is, of course, to acknowledge my having located myself within the geographical local—Ithaca. This is despite, of course, my many protestations against such a locating of myself. All of my protestations show themselves, in one way or another, to be but a kind of willful folly, a benign—but not inconsequential—form of self-denial, if not an obvious form of self-delusion, as if mine were, according to Hamlet, at least, as unconvincing a protestation as Queen Gertrude's.

Hamlet thought himself to be a canny political operator in staging the play within a play, *The Murder of Gonzago* ("The Mousetrap").

He was not. Hamlet was a rank amateur at political machinations, no match for the murderous cunning of his stepfather, Claudius.

It may be that I, like Gertrude, am unable to see what is before me.

Under questioning, I may stand accused by Ezra of defending myself too vigorously. If I am fortunate, the inquiry put to me by Ezra will surely stand as the most gentle of Yeatsian indictments: "The best lack all conviction, while the worst / Are full of passionate intensity."[69]

But I will know that I know Yeats's truth.

Like Gertrude, I fear that I have protested too much—in vain.

What merit can there possibly be to my case? My problem is that I number not among Yeats's "best." It is not "conviction" that I "lack." With my "passionate intensity," which has troubled Nip, Jane, family members, and countless friends, I surely have no choice but to take my place among the Yeatsian "worst."

Mea culpa.

Notes.

1. William Butler (W. B.) Yeats, "Second Coming," in *Collected Poems* (London: MacMillan, 1985), 210.
2. Jeff Kinney, *Diary of a Wimpy Kid: Greg Heffley's Journal* (New York: Amulet, 2007), 1.
3. *The Godfather: Part III*, directed by Francis Ford Coppola (Paramount Pictures, 1990).
4. William Shakespeare, *Hamlet*, act 3, scene 1, line 83 (London: Methuen, 1982).
5. See Roger Kahn, *The Boys of Summer* (New York: Harper Perennial, 2006).
6. Ninety-five Liverpool fans died at Hillsborough and in its immediate aftermath. The ninety-sixth, Tony Bland, died in 1993 due to brain injuries sustained at Hillsborough. In 2019, Andrew Devine, the ninety-seventh victim, died at the age of fifty-five. He had been twenty-two years old when he went to watch that FA Cup semifinal. Devine died of the life-changing injuries he suffered at Hillsborough.
7. Daniel Jones was cut by the Giants in November 2024. Years too late. They should never have drafted him, much less have signed him to a massive four-year extension. I was immensely glad to se the back of "Danny Dimes."
8. In October 2024, the Knicks traded Randle—hooray! is the polite rendering of my exuberance—to the Minnesota Timberwolves. In return, the Knicks got New Jersey native, "KAT" (Karl Anthony Towns). KAT grew up a Knicks fan. He is SO much better than Randle even if he is a terrible rebounder, especially terrible if one considers that he is 7′ tall. Still, he is NOT Randle.
9. Grant Farred, *The Perversity of Gratitude: An Apartheid Education* (Philadelphia: Temple University Press, 2024).
10. The modified principles—and they are principles rather than rules that are strictly followed—apply to every sports code, from basketball to football (what Americans improperly call "soccer") to baseball and so on. Skeptic that I am, I cannot help but wonder: What are they modified from—pure, unadulterated competition? Why are players

who are second stringers guaranteed playing time? Shouldn't that time be earned? Isn't America the land of meritocracy? If the kid's not good enough, maybe they just shouldn't play, unless, as is the case anyway, the game's a blowout one way (the team's winning by a big margin) or the other (the team's so far behind the scoreline has long since become a nonissue).

11. Hisham Matar, *The Return: Fathers, Sons, and the Land In Between* (New York: Random House, 2017).

12. However, since the late-1990s, North Adams has undergone an economic revitalization. The town is now home to MASS MoCA, the Massachusetts Museum of Contemporary Art, which, of course, has been accompanied by the rise in hip coffee shops and the other industries that have come to accompany urban renewal. On a small scale, North Adams now has its own creative class. Attached to Williams College, de facto if not de jure, is the fine Clark Art Institute (known to locals simply as "The Clark"), which has a fine collection of American and European art that covers a broad historical range, from the Renaissance to modern American art. As seems fitting, however, the two museums have a very different emphasis; the Clark's ethos is similar to that of Williams College and the town, while MASS MoCA is geared to the cutting edge.

13. In the decades since I lived there, North Adams has been spruced up quite a bit. Some of the more hip Williams College faculty now make their homes in North Adams.

14. Of course, not all students at elite liberal arts colleges subscribe to the logic of the Williams student I encountered. Many of them choose to attend the likes of Bates, Haverford, Swarthmore, Pomona, and so on because they want to go to more academically intimate institutions that have smaller class sizes and more favorable faculty-to-student ratios. Plus, many of these elite liberal arts colleges are very well endowed financially. And, especially with a place such as Williams, which is geographically isolated, there is an intense sense of community—sometimes too much so, if you ask me, hence the joke about changing light bulbs: "How many Williams students does it take to change a light bulb? All of them. They have nothing else to do." Some of the athletes at elite liberal arts colleges choose these institutions because they will have a better chance of actually playing on the team; opportunities for competing—even just making the team—are much greater at the likes of Carleton or Williams than they would be at a Division I school. However, what struck me about the Williams student's self-designation was his hierarchical insight. Williams for him wasn't Harvard, but that was the only institutional comparison his hierarchy of US education could bear. He wasn't a "Dartmouth reject." The logic? After Harvard comes Williams. Better a Harvard reject than a UPenn alum.

15. See Debra Goldschmidt, "Colleges Come to Terms with Slave-Owning Pasts," CNN, May 23, 2011, http://www.cnn.com/2011/US/05/23/university.slavery/index.html#:~:text=In%202003%2C%20Brown%20University%20became%20one%20of%20the,the%20New%20England%20slave%20trade%20and%20the%20university.

16. Craig Steven Wilder, *Ebony & Ivy: Race, Slavery, and the Troubled History of America's Universities* (New York: Bloomsbury, 2013), 74. Wilder provides an in-depth study of the links between the rise of US higher education and the economy of the slave trade.

17. Wilder, *Ebony & Ivy*, 73.

18. Julie Bosman, "A Princeton Maverick Succumbs to a Cultural Shift," *The New York Times*, January 3, 2007, https://www.nytimes.com/2007/01/03/books/03mica.html.

19. "Coeducation at Princeton University—Women at Princeton—A Brief History," Princeton University Library, February 14, 2024, https://libguides.princeton.edu/coeducation/briefhistory.

20. Butler was traded to the Golden State Warriors in February 2025.

21. For the life of me, I can't imagine who that player would have been. Peter Thompson, maybe, Ian St. John? Salient about that 1965 FA Cup final between Liverpool and Leeds United was that it featured the coloured South African winger Albert Johanneson who played for Leeds. In 1972, Johanneson dropped by the primary (elementary) school I was attending for a coaching session. It is easily the closest I got (physically, anyway) to Bill Shankly. Liverpool beat Leeds 2–1 in extra-time with an Ian St. John header.

22. See Chris Herring, *Blood in the Garden: The Flagrant History of the 1990s New York Knicks* (New York: Atria, 2022). Wonderfully (and appropriately) titled, Herring's book provides an illuminating, at times disturbing, and sometimes hilarious account of Pat Riley's Knicks. This team fought each other at practice in preseason. Anthony Mason emerges as the scariest member of that team.

23. A chapter of *Long Distance Love* is dedicated to my FC Barcelona fandom.

24. I develop the concept first, if only in broad strokes, in *What's My Name?: Black Vernacular Intellectuals* and then fully, as is titularly obvious, in *The Burden of Over-representation: Race, Sport, and Philosophy*. See Farred, *What's My Name?: Black Vernacular Intellectuals* (Minneapolis: University of Minnesota Press, 2003). See Farred, *The Burden of Over-representation: Race, Sport, and Philosophy* (Philadelphia: Temple University Press, 2018).

25. It should be noted that Manchester City have endured a difficult 2024–25 season. They are, on this season's performance, a shadow of their former formidable selves. But they still have Pep.

26. Andy Hunter, "For Bill Shankly in 1974 Read Jürgen Klopp in 2024—But What Comes Next?," *The Guardian*, January 26, 2024, https://www.theguardian.com/football/2024/jan/26/for-bill-shankly-in-1974-read-jurgen-klopp-in-2024-but-what-comes-next.

27. In June 2024, at the age of twenty-three, Dominik Szoboszlai became the youngest player to captain a nation at the European Championships.

28. Countee Cullen, "Yet Do I Marvel," in *My Soul's High Song: The Collected Writings of Countee Cullen*, ed. Gerald Early (New York: Anchor, 1991), 79.

29. Cullen, "Yet Do I Marvel."

30. Taylor Swift, "Style," track 3 on *1989*, Big Machine Records, 2014.

31. "Jurgen Klopp Is 'Officially a Swiftie,'" *NZ Entertainment News*, June 18, 2024, https://home.nzcity.co.nz/news/article.aspx?id=400539.

32. David K. Li, "Aaron Rodgers Injured in First Drive for New York Jets, Who Go On to Improbable OT Win," NBC News, September 12, 2023, https://www.nbcnews.com/news/sports/aaron-rodgers-injured-new-york-jets-rcna104550.

33. Becky Sullivan, "A Taylor Swift Instagram Post Helped Drive a Surge in Voter Registration," NPR, September 22, 2023, https://www.npr.org/2023/09/22/1201183160/taylor-swift-instagram-voter-registration. See also Justine McDaniel, "Taylor Swift Urged People to Register to Vote, and Thousands Did," *The Washington Post*, September 22, 2023, https://www.washingtonpost.com/nation/2023/09/22/taylor-swift-voter-registration/.

34. Julia Reinstein, "Vivek Ramaswamy Pushes Conspiracy about Taylor Swift and Travis Kelce," *Independent*, January 29, 2024, https://www.independent.co.uk/news/world/americas/us-politics/vivek-ramaswamy-taylor-swift-conspiracy-b2486903.html.

35. David Moye, "Vivek Ramaswamy Ridiculed For Taylor Swift Super Bowl Conspiracy," *HuffPost*, January 29, 2024, https://www.huffpost.com/entry/vivek-ramaswamy-taylor-swift-super-bowl_n_65b7eb5ae4b077c17ab607cb.

36. I spoke too soon. The Commanders had a superb 2024 season, losing in the National Football Conference championship game to the Philadelphia Eagles, who, in turn, triumphed over Mahomes and the Chiefs in Super Bowl LIX.

37. See, for example, Debra Utacia Krol, "With Chiefs in the Super Bowl, Some Native People Say It's Time to Erase the Offensive Name," *USA Today*, February 10, 2023, https://www.usatoday.com/story/sports/2023/02/10/native-activists-kansas-city-chiefs-name-mascot-change/11227316002/. See also Leah Asmelash, "How the Kansas City Chiefs Got Their Name, and Why It's So Controversial," CNN, February 1, 2020, https://www.cnn.com/2020/02/01/us/kansas-city-chiefs-name-race-trnd/index.html; Ben Axelrod, "MLB Commissioner Rob Manfred Says Atlanta Braves Can Keep Name, Tomahawk Chop," WKYC Studios, October 27, 2021, https://www.wkyc.com/article/sports/mlb/braves-name-tomahawk-chop-wont-change-mlb/95-1e4c3d3a-80d6-4a0d-8451-9fba40951c60; and Steven Kubitza, "Atlanta Braves Next MLB Team in Line for a Name Change," *Call to the Pen*, July 26, 2021, https://calltothepen.com/2021/07/26/atlanta-braves-next-mlb-team-line-name-change/.

38. He did not.

39. Hank Lee, "Steve Wilks: 'It Was an Honor' to Be Panthers Interim Coach," WCNC Charlotte, January 27, 2023, https://www.wcnc.com/article/sports/nfl/panthers/steve-wilks-first-statement-carolina-panthers-head-coach-position/275-d12fe5b5-c219-47cf-b572-d84e5742192a.

40. See Tashan Reed, "A Shift in Hiring, But Will it Last?" *The New York Times*, June 17, 2024.

41. See Savannah Shange, *Progressive Dystopia: Abolition, Antiblackness, and Schooling in San Francisco* (Durham, NC: Duke University Press, 2019).

42. And Stephen A. Smith agrees. See Steve Zavala, "ESPN Analyst Goes Off 49ers Over Call to Part Ways with Defensive Coordinator Steve Wilks," A to Z Sports, February 16, 2024, https://atozsports.com/nfl/san-francisco-49ers-news/espn-analyst-goes-off-on-49ers-over-call-to-part-ways-with-defensive-coordinator-steve-wilks/. See also Lorenzo Reyna, "Shannon Sharpe, Chard Ochocinco and Others Rip 49ers for Firing Steve Wilks," Pro Football Network, February 17, 2024, https://www.profootballnetwork.com/shannon-sharpe-chad-ochocinco-steve-wilks-nfl-trends-2024/.

43. David Bonilla, "Bayless on 49ers: I Don't Believe in Kyle Shanahan or Brock Purdy," 49ers Webzone, February 18, 2024, https://www.49erswebzone.com/articles/178755-bayless-49ers-believe-shanahan-brock/.

44. Randall Barnes, "49ers Catch Stray from Richard Jefferson during Celebrity All-Star Game Rules Explanation," Clutch Points, February 17, 2024, https://clutchpoints.com/49ers-news-san-francisco-catches-stray-from-richard-jefferson-during-celebrity-all-star-game-rules-explanation.

45. Grant Cohn, "Can Brock Purdy Overcome a Bad Head Coach?" *Sports Illustrated*, February 18, 2024, https://www.si.com/nfl/49ers/news/can-brock-purdy-overcome-a-bad-head-coach. This is a piece that is at once funny and unreflective. On the one hand, it takes Shanahan to task, rightly; on the other, it fails to see the irony of trumpeting Purdy, who it expects will excel, but only under optimal conditions. This begs the question: What moderately capable NFL quarterback wouldn't perform well under optimal conditions, or what the piece labels the "elite" players surrounding Purdy? See also Ryan Gaydos, "'Bad Coaching' Reason for 49ers' Super Bowl LVIII Loss Not Brock Purdy, ex-NFL Star Says," Fox News, February 19, 2024, https://www.foxnews.com/sports/bad-coaching-reason-49ers-super-bowl-lviii-loss-not-brock-purdy-ex-nfl-star-says.

46. I called 9-1-1. The Stoughton police arrived but seemed largely indifferent, a guise they presented as investigative—there were two sides to the story, that was their line, and did they ever stick to it. They took a statement from me, but mine was, in their logic, just one of the accounts to be considered, according to Officer W. How do you, as a specta-

tor, as a parent, as an official, unsee a father-coach choke his son, #5? The Barros team's coach, D. A., denied having choked his son and was backed up by the Barros team parents. Officer W. assured me that he would be obtaining video of the incident in dispute. After a few attempts to reach him, I finally received a call from Officer W. on July 31, 2024, to tell me that no charges would be filed. But he assured me that because of the report, a "paper trail" had been established, and should such an incident occur again ... From my first encounter with Officer W. and his three colleagues (one of whom was Officer B.), I had no faith that the Stoughton Police Department would file charges. Whether that is because the event would have brought disrepute on Dana Barros, former Boston College standout and Boston Celtics player, I cannot say for sure. (The benefit of the local dispute goes to the local benefactor? Or, more specifically, the institution that bears the local benefactor's imprimatur?) Whether or not video evidence actually existed, who knows? Jane and I deliberated as to whether to continue with the tournament. We finally did. I made that decision with a heap of bile in my mouth. Ezra's team, which played the entire tournament without substitutes, had only five players, meaning that if we decided to leave, Nip's team would have had to forfeit. The understanding that I was left with is that in AAU, a team cannot take the court without its full complement of players. But hadn't something far more fundamental already been forgone? I will live with that question.

47. The U2 lyrics evoke an entire literary history. The Latin term, which is not really a Latin term in any discernible sense, *nolite te bastardes carborundorum* (don't let the bastards grind you down), is understood to be a joke by scholars of Latin but the term retains its currency. See, for example, Margaret Atwood's playful but politically astute use of it in the article "*Handmaid's Tale*: The Strange History of 'Nolite te Bastardes Carborundorum,'" available at https://www.vanityfair.com/hollywood/2017/05/handmaids-tale-nolite-te-bastardes-carborundorum-origin-margaret-atwood. Song lyrics available at https://www.azlyrics.com/lyrics/u2band/acrobat.html.

48. As it turns out, AK is going to graduate a year early. He has enough AP credits to do so. This will be a significant loss.

49. Full text available at https://www.ushistory.org/documents/ask-not.htm.

50. See Tom Fleischmann, "Big Red Men Sprinting toward Ivy League Basketball Title," *Cornell Chronicle*, March 12, 2024, https://news.cornell.edu/stories/2024/03/big-red-men-sprinting-toward-ivy-league-basketball-title. It speaks well of Brian Earl that he borrowed not only from Klopp but from the legendary Dutch football coach Rinus Michels, who, in the early 1960s, developed a system of playing called "total football." Michels introduced his philosophy at Ajax, the greatest club in Dutch football, featuring icons such as Johan Cruyff. It involved a style of play that was soon adopted by the Dutch national team, a squad dominated by Ajax stars.

51. There are, however, those proximate to him on the sidelines who suggest that he has some choice things to say, not least of all about his players. My source will remain anonymous.

52. Howard Gayle, "Howard Gayle: I Needed Mental Resilience to Survive as Liverpool's First Black Player," *The Guardian*, October 3, 2016, https://www.theguardian.com/football/2016/oct/03/howard-gayle-being-liverpool-first-black-player-was-difficult. In a training ground conflict between Gayle and Smith, described in this *Guardian* story, when Smith unleashed a torrent of racist invective against Gayle, the only LFC player to support Gayle was Graeme Souness, himself later an LFC captain. Souness is not only one of my favorite LFC players, he is the LFC player—as captain and no-nonsense central midfielder (my position)—I most wanted to emulate. I have a Souey #11 jersey, vintage, from his marauding days as the LFC supremo (the late 1970s to the mid-1980s).

53. Roy Brown was the son of a Nigerian father and an English mother. He played in central defense for Stoke. When Crooks broke into the Stoke City team in the 1975–76 season (making his debut in April 1976), I was completely unaware of Roy Brown. See "Football's Pioneers: Roy Brown," LCFC, May 31, 2021, https://www.lcfc.com/news/2161920/?lang=en. This means that until very recently, I had always thought of Crooksie as the first black player to represent Stoke City.

54. Garth Crooks's Caribbean lineage is strictly, by all accounts, Jamaican, whereas Barnes, as we know, has a Trinidadian father. But Barnes was born in Jamaica. Barnes's father, Ken, was "Jamaica's cultural attaché to London in the late 1970s and early 1980s." See John Barnes, *John Barnes: The Autobiography* (London: Headline, 1999), 2.

55. Mark Chamberlain's older brother is named Neville. Imagine that, a black Briton so named.

56. Both Mark and Alex would represent England on the international stage.

57. Tommy Smith, Phil Thompson, Jamie Carragher, Robbie Fowler, and, of course, Stevie Gerrard. Even for a brief moment, Steve MacMahon. These other Scousers are white. I should also mention Curtis Jones. Like Robbie Fowler, the mixed-race Curtis Jones was born in Toxteth, but Jones has only ever been a stand-in captain. TAA is poised to become *captain*, emulating his hero, Stevie Gerrard—Gerrard coached Jones when the latter was in the Liverpool U-18 team.

58. For an incisive account of the role that Emerson's critique of the United States plays in the history of American philosophy—or, the "evasion" thereof—see Cornel West, *The American Evasion of Philosophy: A Genealogy of Pragmatism* (Madison: University of Wisconsin Press, 1989).

59. Fred Jameson: April 14, 1934–September 22, 2024.

60. Jane, Nip, and I watched the US men's Olympic basketball team play South Sudan twice—once in a warmup game to the Paris Olympics and once in the Paris Olympics itself. The entire project that is South Sudan basketball has been funded by the South Sudanese native Luol Deng. Mr. Deng, as I referred to him then and refer to him still, has financed the South Sudan team and was on the bench as an assistant coach during the Olympics. Hats off to Mr. Deng.

61. Elton John, "Sorry Seems to Be the Hardest Word," track 9 on *Blue Moves*, Rocket Records, 1976.

62. In late June 2024, it was announced that the Knicks had signed OG to a max contract, to the tune of $212 million. OG's a good player, but he is rarely fit for more than fifty-five games or so a season out of an eighty-two-game season, to say nothing of the playoffs. See Jeff Zillgitt, "Knicks Continue to Go All-In as They Launch $212 Million Deal with OG Anunoby," *USA Today*, June 26, 2024, https://www.usatoday.com/story/sports/nba/knicks/2024/06/26/og-anunoby-new-contract-knicks-212-million/74225825007/.

63. The Knicks lost in the Eastern Conference semifinals, 3–4, to the Indiana Pacers. By that stage, the Knicks were down to a bare-bones squad. Not only was Randle injured in the regular season, but in the postseason, Mitchell Robinson, OG, and Bojan Bogdanović were laid low by injury, and Josh Hart and Brunson were playing through injury.

64. Bob Dylan, "Blowin' in the Wind," track 1 on *The Freewheelin' Bob Dylan*, Columbia, 1963.

65. Dylan, "Blowin' in the Wind."

66. Full name: Hobart and Willliam Smith Colleges.

67. William Shakespeare, *Hamlet*, act 3 scene 2 (London: Methuen, 1982).

68. See, among other stories on Earl's resignation, Donna Ditota, "Cornell Men's Basketball Coach Brian Earl Leaves Ithaca and Takes New Head Coaching Job," Syracuse

.com, March 23, 2024, https://www.syracuse.com/sports/2024/03/cornell-mens-basket ball-coach-brian-earl-leaves-ithaca-and-takes-new-head-coaching-job.html. See also W&M Athletics Staff, "William & Mary Selects Brian Earl to Lead Men's Basketball," *W&M News*, March 26, 2024, https://news.wm.edu/2024/03/26/william-mary-selects -brian-earl-to-lead-mens-basketball/.

69. W. B. Yeats, "The Second Coming," *Collected Poems* (London: Macmillan, 1982), 158.

Index.

AC Milan, 86, 158
Affective power, 3, 4
Akron, University of, 203, 204
Alabama, University of, 66, 203
Alexander-Arnold, Trent, xv, 89, 92, 153, 158, 159, 175
Algerian-French philosopher, 194. *See also* Derrida, Jacques
Amateur Athletic Union (AAU), 30, 31, 106, 127, 211n46
Amendments, Thirteenth, Fourteenth, and Fifteenth, 160
Amherst College, 42, 51
Amsterdam Avenue, 9, 176, 177, 180
Anderson, Viv, 156
Anfield (Liverpool FC stadium), 73, 79–81, 111, 156, 159, 164
Anthony, Carmelo, 20, 33, 191
Anunoby, OG, 20, 190, 191, 196, 212n62
Anya, Kalu, 188
Apartheid, 1, 2, 5, 8, 25, 98, 155, 171, 207n9
Arsenal FC, 12, 14, 66, 84, 156, 200
Athleticism, 29, 30, 59
Atlantic, 173
Auburn University, 203
Auto-fascism, 14, 16, 18, 199

Backdoor cuts, 22, 23, 144
Barnes, John, 137, 154–159, 171, 172, 210n44, 212n54
Barrett, RJ, 20, 174, 191
Batson, Brendon, 156
Beccles, Jacob, xiv, 54, 55, 61, 96, 99, 131, 137, 139, 140, 142, 150, 151, 170, 192, 193
Beckenbauer, Franz, 159
Becker, Allison Ramsés, 157
Berlin Wall, 173, 174
Big Green, 47, 95, 130
Big Red, 9, 38, 47, 49, 63, 95, 122, 130, 166, 169, 211n50
Boothby, Keller, xiv, 3, 10, 56, 57, 60, 61, 99, 104, 105, 131, 139, 140, 146, 147, 149, 160, 166, 193, 202
Borussia Dortmund, 83, 88, 202
Boston College, 211
Brooklyn, New York, 52, 58, 192, 203
Brown, Roy, 155, 212n53
Brown University, 45, 49–51, 122, 133, 149, 169, 170, 176, 183, 188, 189, 208n15
Brunson, Jalen, 20, 186, 191, 196, 212n63
Buffalo Bills, 109–112, 199

Cameron Arena, 39, 172
Campbell, Tim, 190

Cape Town, South Africa, 42, 79, 124, 125, 171
Carril, Pete, 22, 23, 26, 27, 144, 145
Chamberlain, Mark, 156, 212n55
Champions League, 11, 12, 85, 87
Chelsea FC, 66, 92, 93, 97
Chicago Bulls, 172, 203
Chicago Cubs, 76, 121, 165
Civil War, 160
Claudius, 205
Coastal Athletic Conference, 202
College of Charleston, 202
Collins, Phil, 135, 186, 187
Communist (Poland), 173
Cornell University, xiii, xiv, 7–9, 25, 37, 38, 39, 45–47, 49, 58, 60, 62, 65, 70, 72, 105, 165
Cornell University Athletics Department, 48, 57, 140, 152, 162
Cornell University Basketball, xiii, 2, 3, 5, 7–10, 20–23, 30, 36, 37, 47, 48, 49, 51–53, 58, 59, 60–63, 65, 76, 77, 82, 95, 96, 104, 105, 122, 123, 130–137, 140, 143–146, 148, 149–152, 166–170, 175, 177–180, 182, 183, 185, 188, 192, 193, 194, 197, 200–205
Columbia University, 25, 45, 46, 64, 133, 137, 148, 165, 170, 176–178
Columbia University's Levien Gym, 165, 176
Crooks, Garth, 155, 156, 212nn53–54
Cunningham, Laurie, 156

Dalglish, Kenny, 13, 79, 80, 90, 154
Dartmouth College, 37, 43, 45–48, 51, 63, 95, 96, 122, 130, 133, 208n14
Deng, Luol, 172, 212n60
Derrida, Jacques, 194
Dewey, John, 165
DJ Nix, 61, 95
Dole, Libby, 172
Du Bois, W. E. B., 160
Dulce et decorum est, 165
Duke University, 27, 30, 39, 95, 127, 172, 174, 175, 203
Duke University Program in Literature, 172
Durham, North Carolina, 173
Durham Bulls, 165
Dylan, Bob, 198–200, 212nn64–65

Earl, Brian, xiii, 2–7, 9, 10, 21–24, 40, 48, 49, 53, 56, 61–63, 67–71, 73, 95, 96, 98, 100, 105, 131, 137, 143–145, 149, 160, 166–168, 170, 172, 175, 180, 182–185, 193, 194, 197, 198, 201, 202–204, 211n50, 212n68
Eastern and Central Europe, 173
Emerson, Ralph Waldo, 51, 164, 165, 212n58
Estadio Wanda Metropolitano, 157
European Union of Football Associations (EUFA), 155
Everton FC, 66, 154
Ezra "Nip" Farred, xiii, xiv, 1–3, 6, 8, 15, 20–24, 29–34, 35, 36, 51, 52, 54, 61–63, 76, 77, 82, 97, 99, 100, 102, 106, 123, 124, 127, 135, 137, 146, 174, 177, 203, 205, 211n46

FA Cup (Football Association Cup), 12, 13, 79, 81, 90, 207n6, 209n21
FC Barcelona, 85, 90, 209n23
Fiegen, Jake, 61, 130, 131, 137, 138–142, 149, 160, 161, 166–168, 172, 178, 182, 185, 192
Fisk University, 160
Fitzgerald, F. Scott, 67, 68
Frazier, Walt Clyde, 62, 71, 169

Gasser, Patrick, 155
Gayle, Howard, 154, 158, 159, 211n52
Gdansk, Poland, 173
Geneva, New York, 201
George Washington University, 202, 204
Gerrard, Steven George, 102, 103, 159, 212n57
"GQ," 168
Gray, Isaiah "Zeke," xiv, 3, 6, 7, 10, 21, 24, 31, 35–37, 47–52, 56, 61–63, 95, 96, 99, 100, 104, 105, 131, 135, 137, 139, 143–146, 148, 149–152, 162, 163, 166–169, 172, 179, 180, 182, 192–194, 197, 198, 203, 204

Hamlet, 205, 207n4, 212n67
Hanover, New Hampshire, 43, 46–48, 124–126
Hansen, Sean, xiv, 3, 10, 53, 61–63, 76, 104, 105, 131, 144, 145, 148, 152, 166, 167, 169, 172, 179, 180, 192, 193, 202
Hardt, Michael, 172
Hart, Josh, xv, 3, 186, 190, 191, 196, 212n63
Harvard University, 38, 39, 42, 45, 48, 58, 63, 67, 95, 104, 122, 133, 148, 160, 174, 208n14
Heffley, Greg, 1, 197, 207n2
Hegel, G. W. F., 17
Heysel Stadium, 13, 14, 200
Hillsborough Disaster (1989), 13, 14, 80, 200, 207n6

Hinton, Adam Tsang, 61, 96, 131, 147
Hobart College, 201, 212n66
Hughes, Emlyn, 154

Ince, Paul, 158
Ivy League, 38, 39, 46, 50, 65, 68
Ivy League Basketball, 5, 21, 21–24, 39, 49, 53, 132, 138, 139, 148, 170, 189, 203, 211n50
Ivy Madness, 5, 177, 183, 204

Jameson, Fred, 172, 212n59
Jaques, Jon, xiii, 3, 7, 21, 31, 100, 131, 134–137, 148, 170, 172, 175, 178, 183, 204
"Jersey Legend," 201
Jones, Daniel, 19, 207n7
Jones, James, 52, 104, 168, 189

Kaczyński, Lech, 173
Kahn, Roger, 9, 32, 179, 207n5
Kaepernick, Colin, 117, 121, 165
Kansas City Chiefs, 20, 106, 107, 114, 115, 121, 174, 210n37
Kerber, Chris, 201
Klopp, Jürgen, 4, 7, 13, 73–76, 79–86, 88–91, 94, 97, 98, 101, 111, 143, 155, 156, 159, 194, 202, 204, 209n26, 31, 211n50
Knowling, Matt, 166, 188, 189
Krzyzewski, Mike (Coach K), 172–175

Lansur Untied, 126
Law and Justice Party (Poland), 173
Lech Wałęsa's Solidarity Movement, 173
Leeds United FC, 14, 209n21
Leonard, Kawhi, 30, 190
Lilly, Kino, Jr., 188, 189
Liverpool Football Club (LFC), xiv, xv, 1, 2, 7–18 20, 22, 24, 55, 66, 73–75, 79–83, 85–93, 97, 101, 102, 153–159, 164, 171, 172, 175, 180, 198–200, 207n6, 209n21, 211n52, 212n57
Liverpool John Moores University, 172
Los Angeles Dodgers, 9

Mahoney, August, 166, 168, 189
Manchester (Man) City, 55, 83, 87, 90, 91, 209n25
Manchester United FC, 12, 66, 84, 87, 101
Manningham, Mario, 199
Manon, Chris, xiv, 10, 31, 47, 51–53, 58–63, 99, 100, 104, 105, 122, 130, 131, 137, 139, 144, 145, 151, 152, 167, 172, 179, 194, 198, 202
March Madness, 5, 21, 22
Mason, Anthony, 32, 62, 82, 209n22
Mbeng, Bez, 52, 151, 166–168, 188, 189
Melwood, 158
Miami Dolphins, 20, 110
Miami Heat, 77
Mitch Henderson, 22, 53, 71, 157, 168, 183
Mohair Brigade, 173
Moi, Toril, 172
Mudimbe, V. Y., 172
The Murder of Gonzago ("The Mousetrap"), 205

Nashville, Tennessee, 160, 202
National anthem, 89, 164, 165
National Collegiate Athletic Association (NCAA), 5, 6, 21, 22, 78, 135, 144, 169, 170, 174
National Hockey League, 199
National Invitational Tournament (NIT), 179, 185, 192, 204
Newman Arena, 7, 47, 49, 53, 104, 105, 132, 142, 143, 164
New York Giants, 18, 19, 62, 175, 199, 207n7
New York Knicks, xv, 3, 8, 19, 20, 30–33, 52, 58, 59, 62, 71, 77, 78, 82, 123, 169, 174, 175, 186, 190, 191, 196–200, 207n8, 209n22, 212nn62–63
New York Mets, 18, 76, 175, 198, 199
New York Rangers, 199
Noard, Cooper, 56, 61, 122, 130, 131, 169, 192
Nottingham Forest, 13, 156

Ohio State University Buckeyes, 145, 179, 185, 192, 193, 203, 204
Okereke, AK, 56, 130
Ontology, 198, 200
Owen, Wilfred, 165
Owusu-Anane, Nana, 188
Oxlade-Chamberlain, Alex, 156

Paisley, Bob, 79, 80, 89, 90
Pennsylvania, University of Basketball, 39, 45, 50, 51, 130, 133, 134, 148, 168, 170, 108
Pope John Paul II, 173
Port Vale, 156
Poulakidas, John, 189
Premier League, 2, 5, 12, 15, 16, 55, 75, 83, 87, 90, 97, 155, 164

Princeton University Basketball, 22, 23, 26, 36, 37, 39, 53, 56, 58, 60, 61, 63, 63, 65, 67–71, 77, 105, 131–134, 143, 144, 148, 166, 168–170, 176, 183, 188, 197, 208nn18–19
Princeton University Tigers, 39, 65, 66, 71, 144, 170
Pyongyang, North Korea, 203

Queen Gertrude, 205

Ragland, Guy, xiv, 47, 52, 54, 61, 95, 131, 137, 139–142, 148, 161, 166, 167–169, 172, 178, 183, 192
Randle, Julius, 20, 33, 77, 82, 186, 190, 191, 196, 207n8, 212n63
Real Madrid, 11, 86
Regis, Cyrille, 156
Riley, Pat, 32, 33, 77, 78, 209n22
Rodman, Denis, 15, 203
Rosmead Sports Ground, 124–126

Salt-N-Peppa, 155
Satriani, Joe, 199
Scorcher, 171
Selfish Gene (SG), 102, 103, 182 189
Shankly, Bill, 15, 79, 80, 89, 90, 91, 126, 127, 154, 209n21, 209n26
Shoot, 171
Smith, Dean, 174
Smith, Tommy, 153, 154, 174, 211n52, 212n57
South Africa, 5, 8, 25, 42, 79, 98, 125, 155, 171, 209n21
Staffordshire, 155, 156
Star-Spangled Banner, 164
Stephanians United (Stephs), 125
Stoke-on-Trent (Stoke City), 155, 156, 212n53
Stratford-upon-Avon, 155
Surin, Ken, 172
Syracuse, New York, 3, 11, 204, 212n68

Thomas, Mickey, 200
Thompson, Stefan, 201
Three Degrees, 156
Tiger, 171
Tottenham Hotspur FC (Spurs), 155, 156
Tranmere Rovers, 154
Tribalism, 55, 66
Tyree, David, 199

United States Constitution, 160
University of North Carolina (UNC), 30, 127, 174

Vanderbilt University, 202, 204
Van Dijk, Virgil, 158, 159
Victoria Ground, 156

Wall Street Journal, 172
Washington, Booker T, 160
West Bromwich Albion, 156
West Derby, 158, 159
West Point, 174
William & Mary, the College of, 10, 50, 175, 194, 202, 204, 213n68
Williams, Nazier "Nas," xiv, 3, 31, 36, 47, 48, 53–55, 59–61, 63, 64, 99, 100, 122, 130, 131, 137, 139, 140, 142, 145, 146, 148, 149, 152, 160, 166–160, 172, 177, 179, 182, 183, 192, 193, 198, 202, 203
Williamsburg, 204
Wimbledon FC, 12, 200
Wolff, Danny, 104, 132, 189
World War I, 165
World War II, 88

Yale University Basketball, 37, 49, 52, 67, 95, 96, 104, 105, 122, 131, 132–134, 148, 162, 169, 177–179, 188, 189, 192, 204
Yeats, W. B., 205, 207n1, 213n69

Zen meister, 71, 190

Grant Farred is the author of *Long Distance Love: A Passion for Football*; *The Burden of Over-representation: Race, Sport, and Philosophy*; and *The Perversity of Gratitude: An Apartheid Education*, and the editor of *Africana Studies: Theoretical Futures* (all Temple).

www.ingramcontent.com/pod-product-compliance
Lightning Source LLC
Chambersburg PA
CBHW020946230426
43666CB00005B/187